T0323711

Elements in the Economics of Emerging Markets
edited by
Bruno S. Sergi
Harvard University

THE EMERGING ECONOMIES UNDER THE DOME OF THE FOURTH INDUSTRIAL REVOLUTION

Mark Esposito
Hult International Business School and Harvard University's Division of Continuing Education

Amit Kapoor
Institute for Competitiveness

CAMBRIDGE
UNIVERSITY PRESS

CAMBRIDGE
UNIVERSITY PRESS

University Printing House, Cambridge CB2 8BS, United Kingdom

One Liberty Plaza, 20th Floor, New York, NY 10006, USA

477 Williamstown Road, Port Melbourne, VIC 3207, Australia

314–321, 3rd Floor, Plot 3, Splendor Forum, Jasola District Centre, New Delhi – 110025, India

103 Penang Road, #05–06/07, Visioncrest Commercial, Singapore 238467

Cambridge University Press is part of the University of Cambridge.

It furthers the University's mission by disseminating knowledge in the pursuit of education, learning, and research at the highest international levels of excellence.

www.cambridge.org
Information on this title: www.cambridge.org/9781009095105
DOI: 10.1017/9781009092142

© Mark Esposito and Amit Kapoor 2022

First published 2022

A catalogue record for this publication is available from the British Library.

ISBN 978-1-009-09510-5 Paperback
ISSN 2631-8598 (online)
ISSN 2631-858X (print)

The Emerging Economies under the Dome of the Fourth Industrial Revolution

Elements in the Economics of Emerging Markets

DOI: 10.1017/9781009092142
First published online: July 2022

Mark Esposito
Hult International Business School and Harvard University's Division of Continuing Education

Amit Kapoor
Institute for Competitiveness

Author for correspondence: Mark Esposito, mark@mark-esposito.com

Abstract: The Fourth Industrial Revolution (4IR) is reshaping the globe at a rate far quicker than earlier revolutions. It is also having a greater influence on society and industry. We are currently witnessing extraordinary technology such as self-driving cars and 3D printing, as well as robots that can follow exact instructions. And hitherto unconnected sectors are combining to achieve unfathomable effects. It is critical to comprehend this new era of technology since it will significantly alter life during the next several years in this age of technological advancement. In particular, one of the most significant findings is that 4IR technologies must be used responsibly and to benefit people, companies, and countries as a whole; as a result, the development of artificial intelligence, the Internet of Things, blockchain, and robotics systems will be advanced most effectively by grouping a multidisciplinary team from areas such as computer science, education, and social sciences.

Keywords: Fourth Industrial Revolution (4IR), emerging economies, global value chains (GVC), data giants, Internet of Things (IoT), big data

ISBNs: 9781009095105 (PB), 9781009092142 (OC)
ISSNs: 2631-8598 (online), 2631-858X (print)

Contents

1 Summary

The executive chairman of the World Economic Forum (WEF) said that 'The fourth industrial revolution is not merely a series of incremental technological advancements, it is an upheaval – a dramatic and wide-ranging shift in the way that value is created, exchanged, and distributed across individuals, organizations, and entire economies' (Schwab, 2016; Ally & Wark, 2020).

The 4IR is reshaping the globe at a rate that is far quicker than earlier revolutions. It is also having a greater influence on society and industry. We are currently witnessing extraordinary technology such as self-driving cars and 3D printing, as well as robots that can follow exact instructions. And hitherto unconnected sectors are combining to achieve unfathomable effects. It is critical to comprehend this new era of technology since it will significantly alter life during the next several years in this age of technological advancement.

In particular, one of the most significant findings is that 4IR technologies must be used responsibly and to benefit people, companies, and countries as a whole; as a result, the development of artificial intelligence, the Internet of Things, blockchain, and robotics systems will be advanced most effectively by grouping a multidisciplinary team from areas such as computer science, education and social sciences, ethics, privacy, and security.

The previous industrial revolutions had significant societal ramifications. Steam power and machines, as well as other innovations, have had a tremendous impact on transportation and agriculture throughout history. The 4IR technologies are making significant improvements in business and industry, and they are also having an impact on education. The education sector must make the transition to the 4IR age, or else the business sector will step in to fill the void left by the education sector. Teachers, students, and employees must become familiar with the many types of 4IR technologies in order to be able to perform successfully in the 4IR and contribute to the attainment of Sustainable Development Goals (SDGs). Far from being science fiction, 4IR technologies, including holograms and virtual interactions, are very much a reality (Mavrikios et al., 2019; Pates, 2020).

Schwab, in his book *The Fourth Industrial Revolution* (2017), defined the 4IR as 'a range of new technologies that are fusing the physical, digital, and biological worlds, impacting all disciplines, economies, and industries, and even challenging ideas about what it means to be Human'. The power and varieties of digital gadgets, computer devices, and networks are continuously expanding owing to breakthroughs in the newest technical developments. This facilitates access to education and other forms of knowledge. The gradual growth of technology and scientific advances is resulting in the formation of new educational fields, which, in turn, is resulting in additional changes. The 4IR is improving the opportunities for the creation and invention of new skills. The 4IR stresses the expansion of knowledge and the desire to study. Application-oriented courses are preferred over bookish education. Online social media platforms such as Twitter, LinkedIn, and Facebook are growing increasingly popular as a result of continual technological advancement. Through these social media platforms, anyone may readily communicate and promote their thoughts on any current issue or event in front of the world.

Land is not required for the construction of marketplaces. Online shopping sites and fast delivery services make commodities more accessible at home while also enhancing economic rewards. Customers are also given informed advice via online customer support representatives. The world is becoming a global village, with billions of people and things readily available. Progress in medical sciences, neurosciences, and other fields is leading to healthier lifestyles, enhanced intellectual and mental aptitude, and longer lifespans as a result of the 4IR. The 4IR has an impact on agriculture as well. Crop yields can be increased with the use of bioengineering. Measuring crop populations and detecting weeds or plant pests are also becoming more accessible with the assistance of robots driven by artificial intelligence. Herbicide application can also be done with robotic sprayers.

Carbon emissions, road deaths, and insurance costs are being reduced as a result of breakthroughs in car safety brought about by the 4IR's increasing technology. People no longer need to stand on the side of the road waiting for transportation; instead, they may reserve automobiles or vehicles online and have them brought to their house. Autonomous or driverless cars are also accessible as a result of the 4IR and will reach their peak as technology advances. People no longer need to go to banks for transactions or other critical tasks because of online banking. The majority of bank work may be done from home.

With all these positive impacts of the 4IR, there exist negative impacts as well. Human beings' willingness to use their own intelligence and physical strength is waning as a result of an over-reliance on technology. The use of social media is increasing the gap between a person and their family members, as well as between a person and the rest of society. The virtual world is becoming much more appealing than the actual world, which is causing a social rift to develop. Social media is not always beneficial since it is a platform for disseminating news, some of which may be fake. In the 4IR, individuals' privacy is no longer completely private, because of technical breakthroughs that have enabled tracking systems to be more accurate and efficient. Every action of a human being may be tracked using digital equipment such as CCTV cameras, smartphones, and other similar gadgets. Social media platforms, such as Facebook, Twitter, and other similar platforms, as well as online shopping websites, such as Flipkart, Amazon, and other similar platforms, collect every piece of information about an individual, from their name and date of birth to their credit card or bank details, before allowing them to create a profile or account.

In addition to cyberbullying and hate speech, there are additional negative effects of social media that are steadily becoming more prevalent in the 4IR; because of the increasing improvement in internet connectivity, cyber assaults are also a possibility. However, it should not be forgotten that hacking is not always ethical and that it might have negative consequences for the overall security of people as well as of government institutions. Going to the market, jogging under the open sky, or visiting someone's house are examples of the activities that people find less appealing since technology advancements have allowed them to buy online, jog on treadmills, and communicate with others through social media, among other things. Because of the convenience of smart technology, children are more interested in mobile games than they are in outdoor games. This has a negative impact on human health, both physically and mentally, as the mobility of the human body and the intake of fresh air are both reduced as a result. Children's physical and mental development is being hampered by their excessive usage of smartphones and digital games.

Because of developments in automotive and robotic technologies, the breadth of work is being threatened. In the face of artificial intelligence, human abilities are becoming increasingly devalued. Machines are given preferential treatment over human beings. Constantly rising concentrations of wealth among a limited number of people are seen. Because of this, individuals are becoming economically and socially inequitable. Inevitable consequences of this include social disintegration, political division, and a loss of faith in institutions. One of the detrimental consequences of the 4IR is global climate change. Fast technological advancement, rising urbanisation, excessive deforestation, infinite resource depletion, desertification, rapid population expansion, water shortages, food insecurity, and other factors are interfering with the natural environmental balance of our planet. Population movement for greater opportunities and concentration in one location, while leaving another isolated, puts pressure on one area of the world while the other continues to grow at a slower pace than the first region. This results in environmental imbalance as well as unequal global development, which in turn results in social inequality throughout the world. Inequality is increasing, which may lead to disputes, societal tensions, and violent extremism.

The pace, size, and influence of change on the whole earth that has occurred as a result of the 4IR are unmatched in the history of humanity. The challenges and uncertainties associated with the current technological paradigm of human growth, as well as its societal costs, repercussions, and paradoxes, are all significant factors in human development. The development of new business models based on demand and supply information platforms, the strengthening of the State's control over society and individuals, a dramatic shift in the processes of the State's engagement with civil society, the growth of competition and decentralisation of power, the development of artificial intelligence – all of these can lead to considerable progress in the development and the degeneration of society. A positive trend in the development of society is achievable, provided that the State authorities are capable of adapting to the new conditions that have arisen as a result of the digital revolution.

2 Literature Review

In an increasingly technology-driven world of smart devices, quantum computing, and autonomous vehicles, significant changes are taking place which are challenging long-standing assumptions about the very nature of work and the roles that humans will play in the workforce of the future.

(Schwab, 2016)

While study into the future of work and workforce requirements is still in its infancy and evolution, available literature indicates that job activities, skill requirements, and labour pool composition will all change dramatically as a result of the present socio-economic developments. While past industrial revolutions were also marked by increased automation of job activities, the pace of change in the 4IR is unmatched.

The 4IR is a combination of emerging technologies that is shaping the way we live and work. The Internet of Things (IoT), cloud computing, big data, robotics, artificial intelligence (AI), 3D printing, augmented reality (AR), virtual reality (VR), nanotechnology, and biotechnology are the technologies that are gaining more prominence during the twenty-first century and are overlapping and fusing with one another in this age of innovation. The emerging and developing economies as compared with developed countries have been lagging behind in terms of adoption of the technologies and embracing the 4IR fully.

Specifically, the 4IR proposes a technique to generate a change from machine-dominated to digital production contingent primarily on the overlapping of a plethora of technologies. Because the implementation and applications of related theorems and definitions outlined for the 4IR are not yet mature enough for the majority of real-life implementations, a systematic approach for conducting appropriate assessments and evaluations appears to be urgently required for those countries, industries, societies, establishments, and institutions that wish to accelerate this transformation and adopt it in a significant manner to be fruitful and gainful.

The 4IR scenarios that are well defined, as well as technical infrastructures which include physical systems and management models, are now the primary responsibility of the research community in order to simplify the lives of practitioners. The following seven areas are believed to be vital for the improvement of the industrial sector around the world:

- digital technology, virtualisation, and the IoT
- additive manufacturing (3D printing)
- automation, robotics, AR, VR
- composites, novel materials, and assembly
- controlling and monitoring situations
- human aspect in manufacturing facilities
- efficient and sustainable use of energy.

Despite the fact that many of these breakthroughs are still in their infancy, they are already approaching a critical juncture in their evolution as they build on and magnify one another through the integration of technologies from the physical, digital, and biological worlds. Securing the full economic and social advantages of innovation will be critical to re-establishing a more stable economy and stimulating economic growth and productivity in the future. Unleashing innovation will also help us to address some of the most important issues facing the world today, such as climate change, cybersecurity, and public health, among other things. To achieve these goals, it will be necessary to establish policy frameworks that are fit for purpose and in which innovation may flourish while also ensuring safety, quality, and efficiency. While the profound uncertainty surrounding the development and adoption of emerging technologies means that we do not yet know how the transformations driven by the 4IR will unfold, their complexity and interconnectedness across sectors imply that all stakeholders of global society – governments, business, academia, and civil society – have a responsibility to collaborate to better understand the emerging trends.

Klaus Schwab said,

> The world is experiencing an economic and political upheaval that will continue for the foreseeable future. The forces of the Fourth Industrial Revolution have ushered in a new economy and a new form of globalization,

both of which demand new forms of governance to safeguard the public good. Whether it will improve the human condition will depend on whether corporate, local, national and international governance can adapt in time.

(Schwab, 2018b)

Shared understanding is especially important if we are to construct a collaborative future that reflects shared goals and values. We need a comprehensive and internationally shared understanding of how technology is affecting our lives and the lives of future generations, as well as how it is redefining the economic, social, cultural, and human context in which we live.

3 Introduction

The rise of the 4IR in the emerging economies will profoundly transform the nature of competition and how a country's performance will be measured (Schwab, 2016). Faced with the challenge of becoming data colonies and not data giants, emerging economies stand on a unique cornerstone of opportunity to bypass the conventional laws of competitiveness and leapfrog into the twenty-first century, leading the way to a more equitable form of economic development, under the dome of the 4IR.

The term *Fourth Industrial Revolution*, abbreviated as *4IR* or *Industry 4.0*, was coined by Klaus Schwab, founder and executive chairman of the WEF. He describes those individuals in the 4IR who move between digital domains and offline reality with the use of connected technology to enable and manage their lives (Miller, 2016). The adoption of the digital world has created a fusion of technologies, which makes it difficult to achieve clear-cut segregation of physical, digital, and biological spheres (Schwab, 2015).

As we speak, the 4IR is already underway, one that will be unlike any other that has come before. The 4IR or Industry 4.0 is an amalgamation of various cutting-edge technologies, disruptive in nature and trends, which are transforming the current and developing the new living and work environment that will, in turn, shape the world. The speed of technological breakthroughs, the rate at which the fusion of technologies is taking place, the pervasiveness of the scope of the 4IR, and the cascading impact on the living and work environment will impact the future of work and businesses. As with the previous industrial revolutions, along with economic growth it brings upheavals in the work environment, societal denials and apprehensions, challenges of governance and policies, and a sense of despair in low-skilled workers.

The 4IR opens up windows of opportunity for the emerging countries and it is yet to be seen how effectively this is embraced by the developing and emerging nations – who do not want to lag behind their counterparts, the developed nations, on the path of growth – to reap the benefits of this industrial revolution and foster their economic growth as well as leapfrogging ahead on the trajectory of development.

Technological breakthroughs are being made at a rate that has never been seen before and are touching every industry all over the world (Ægisdóttir, 2016). This technological journey will surely raise red flags about the challenges likely to be encountered in embracing the technologies and impact on societal levels, including work environment, jobs security, and the interaction between pivotal players like policymakers, technocrats, corporate and business houses, and employees.

For the first time, unlike in previous industrial revolutions where technology worked alongside people to improve human activities and make them more productive, 'Industry 4.0 represents a paradigm shift that, albeit partially, is not limited to working alongside but in certain activities replaces human beings' (Senate of the Italian Republic, 2017).

We are on the cusp of a technology revolution that will drastically transform the way we live, work, and interact with one another in the coming years and decades. This transition is unprecedented in terms of its extent, scale, and complexity, and it is unlike anything else humankind has ever witnessed. No one knows exactly how it will evolve, but one thing is certain: the reaction must be coordinated and comprehensive, bringing together all players in the global political system, from the public and corporate sectors to academia and civil society.

The 4IR possesses three characteristics that distinguish it from all preceding revolutions. These traits are as follows:

i. *Rate.* The rate at which contemporary innovations are occurring has never been seen before in history. In contrast to earlier revolutions, the 4IR is growing at an exponential rather than a linear rate. To put things in perspective, it took 119 years for the spindle, a symbol of the First Industrial Revolution, to reach Europe, but the Internet reached every corner of the globe in less than a decade. Aside from that, 1.3 billion people, or 17 per cent of the world's population, are still without access to electricity, which was the cornerstone of the Second Industrial Revolution, and 4 billion people, or a whopping 52 per cent of the world's population, are still without access to the Internet, which is a major concern. The 4IR, on the other hand, took only a little more than three years to successfully infiltrate every element of our daily lives.

ii. *Fusion.* The 4IR builds on the digital revolution and brings together a variety of technologies, creating a fusion that is causing enormous paradigm transformations in the economy, industry, society, and governance. It is not only altering the 'what' and 'how' of things, but it is also altering 'who' we are. Infinite possibilities exist as a result of billions of people being linked through mobile devices that have unparalleled computing power, storage capacity, and access to information. And new technological developments in disciplines like AI, robots, the IoT, autonomous cars, 3D printing, nanotechnology, biotechnology, materials science, energy storage, and quantum computing will multiply these possibilities even further.

iii. *Penetration*. In contrast to its predecessors, the 4IR is not only affecting specific sectors of industry or commerce, but is also affecting entire systems, both across and within countries, industries, and society as a whole. The 4IR is penetrating all the domains – physical, digital, and biological – and all the sectors. Artificial intelligence is already all around us, in everything from self-driving vehicles and drones to virtual assistants and software that translates or invests in foreign currencies. In recent years, significant advances in AI have been achieved, fuelled by exponential growth in processing power and the availability of large amounts of data. These advancements range from software used to identify new pharmaceuticals to algorithms used to forecast our cultural preferences. The biological environment is always engaging with digital manufacturing technologies, which are in a constant state of flux. The fields of computational design, additive manufacturing, materials engineering, and synthetic biology are being combined to create a symbiotic relationship between microorganisms, our bodies, the products we eat, and even the buildings we live in, according to engineers, designers, and architects.

This Element is the result of a research project that has used largely qualitative data from a review of relevant literature. The research study was used because the focus of the study is more on description and explanation rather than prediction (Merriam, 1988).

4 Evolution of Industrial Revolutions and Fusion of Technologies in the 4IR

The term 'revolution' refers to a period of sudden and drastic change. History has witnessed revolutions when new technology and fresh ways of viewing the world caused a significant shift in the functioning of economic systems and social structures. Industry 4.0 was coined for the first time publicly in 2011 by a group of professionals from diverse professions. The German federal government endorsed the concept of a 'High-Tech Strategy for 2020'. A working group of specialists was organised to give more guidance on the concept's applicability, functioning, and implementation.

Industry 4.0 is also referred to as the Fourth Industrial Revolution, and it is built on the 'Internet of Things and services', following mechanisation (Industry 1.0), mass production (Industry 2.0), and automation (Industry 3.0). The IoT is already ingrained in manufacturing in developed countries, particularly in sophisticated manufacturing and service industries such as automobile manufacturing, aircraft manufacturing, insurance, logistics, and also the communications industry (Haller et al., 2008; Bandyopadhyay & Sen, 2011; Rüßmann et al., 2015; Trappey et al., 2017; Hofmann & Rüsch, 2017; Witkowski, 2017).

4.1 Evolution of Industrial Revolutions

The *First Industrial Revolution* was characterised by the transition of hand production methods to mechanised factory systems leading to mass production of goods, textile manufacturing, and the development of roads and canals for transport. It was fuelled primarily by the use of steam engines in locomotives, ships, and machines in factories. It is James Watt who holds the credit for improvements in the development of the steam engine during this period. The First Industrial Revolution began in the late eighteenth century in Britain, soon spreading to continental Europe and the USA, and ended in the mid-nineteenth century. Following the introduction of the steam machine into industries, labour transitioned from being entirely manual to being primarily machine-based. Cotton spinning machines were introduced into textile mills. It wasn't until 1819, when the Cotton Mills and Factories Act was passed, that things began to calm down significantly. Many factory acts followed, giving workers more rights.

The *Second Industrial Revolution* was characterised by massive steel production, electrification allowing assembly line and mass production in manufacturing methods, and large-scale laying of railroads leading to cheap and fast transportation. The primary focus was on steel production, automobiles, electrification, chemicals, and petroleum. In a nutshell, the second revolution was the outburst of steel, chemicals, electricity, and petroleum. The Second Industrial Revolution began in the late nineteenth century and the beginning of World War I marked its end. In this period of history, Henry Ford, the founder of Ford Motors, is credited with being the first to introduce the assembly line to the globe. As a result, there was a significant rise in output, and assembly lines were soon found in practically every industry.

The *Third Industrial Revolution* started in the mid-twentieth century and was characterised by the use of electronics, computers, and digital machines, leading to the world of automation and digitisation, the discovery and use of nuclear energy, explorations in outer space, and the invention of the Internet, marking the breakthrough of a new era of industrialisation. It brought forth the digital revolution and significant advancements in telecommunication, biotechnology, outer space, and automobiles. This is where the automated assembly line became a reality and machines increasingly started replacing people on the factory floor (Ægisdóttir, 2016).

The *Fourth Industrial Revolution (4IR* or *Industry 4.0*) already started emerging at the turn of the twenty-first century, overlapping with the Third Industrial Revolution and building upon it with advancements in several domains. The 4IR is a fusion, an amalgamation of technological break-throughs in AI, AR, VR, nanotechnology, robotics, 3D printing, ADP (Advanced Digital Production), and the IoT. As it has been put aptly by someone, 'The 4IR is a way of describing the blurring of boundaries between the physical, digital and biological worlds' (McGinnis, 2020). The 4IR or Industry 4.0 is rewriting the rules of manufacturing, infrastructure develop-ments, domestic reforms, and trade liberalisation in order to keep pace with the changing times.

4.2 Fusion of Technologies in the 4IR

The 4IR is not a single technology driving the revolution but is a cluster of different technologies that are de facto agglomerated by technological leaders, pivotal users, system integrators, and government policymakers (Martinelli et al., 2019). It is clearly a complex fusion of technologies all connected by cloud-based internet (see Figure 1).

Under the overall domain of the 4IR are some of the cutting-edge technolo-gies that will shape the future impacting tremendously the way of functioning of businesses and the governments and how the individuals and the societies live, work, and interact with each other and the environment. A few such high-end technologies are AI, big data, the IoT, robotics, VR, AR, 5G, and deep learning (DL) . The relevance of these technologies in the 4IR is touched on very briefly below:

i. *Internet of Things (IoT).* One of the most important developments in the 4IR, the IoT is a natural extension of prior levels of connectivity achieved by the Internet to include physical objects and systems. The IoT consists of digital technologies, sensors, communication modules, and software applications which enable everyone to integrate digitally and bring everyone onto the digital platform. It delivers readily available information at your fingertips, which saves uptime and provides the most accurate information. The IoT entails devices with self-identification capabilities, localisation status, data acquisition, and implementation, which are connected via standard

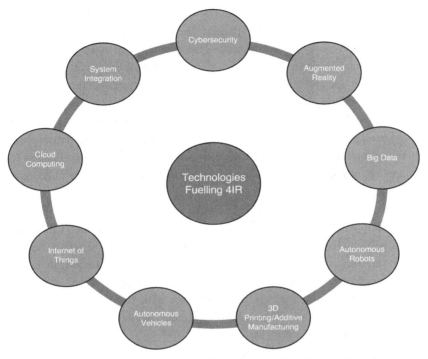

Figure 1 Various technologies fuelling the Fourth Industrial Revolution

communication protocols. IoT technologies are used in manufacturing, housing and construction, automotive, environment, smart city, agriculture, and health applications. In relation to the 4IR, IoT applications are specific to the Industrial Internet of Things (IIoT). As products are becoming connected and commoditised through the IoT, the 4IR will transform the value proposition of businesses from products to the intended outcome of the products.

ii. *Big data*. Some experts say that big data is the 4IR and Industry 4.0. Data is the lifeline of the 4IR. The three key components of big data are volume, variety, and velocity. Big data includes methods and tools to process large volumes of data for manufacturing, supply chain management, and maintenance as well as understanding, analysing, and predicting numerous other things including consumers' behaviour towards products, better customer experiences, patterns of supply and demand, people's/vendors'/suppliers' capabilities of repaying loans, better operational efficiency, improved decision-making, etc. The data can come from IoT systems connected to the productive layer or the exchange between IT systems for production and warehouse management. Specific applications in this area are machine learning tools for planning and forecasting, predictive maintenance, and simulation.

iii. *Cloud technologies*. Experts in Industry 4.0 firms believe that cloud technology is a critical enabler of the 4IR. The true potential of the cloud in support of the 4IR can only be determined via the integration of computing services with a cloud platform. Cloud computing is effectively supporting the developments in the IoT, automation, and robotics. It encompasses the application in manufacturing of cloud technologies, with widespread access, easy and on-demand services – infrastructure, platform, or application – to support processes in supply chain management. Cloud manufacturing ranges from the virtualisation of physical resources necessary for factory equipment to applications, data, and processes across platforms, and execution and collaboration tools hosted in the cloud.

iv. *Robotics*. The robotics cluster includes SCARA (Selective Compliance Articulated Robot Arm), Articulated, Cartesian, Dual Arm and Co-BOTS (collaborative robots responding to human instructions and actions unlike autonomous robots), as different ways to automate production tasks. Advanced automation encompasses the latest developments in production systems with improved ability to interact with the environment, self-learning and automatic guidance, and the use of vision and pattern recognition.

v. *Artificial intelligence (AI)*. This concerns the knowledge and techniques developed to make machines intelligent, that is to say to function appropriately through foresight in their environment of the application. Industrial AI refers to the computer-science-based technologies which, coupled with machine learning, are used to generate intelligent sensors, edge computing, and smart production systems.

vi. *Additive manufacturing*. Also known as 3D printing, this consists of production by depositing layer upon layer of material in exact geometric shapes. Additive manufacturing finds applications in the prototyping (to support the product development process, static simulation, wind tunnel, etc.) manufacturing (direct production of products), maintenance and repairs, and modelling phases.

In short, there are *three core components to the transformation* needed to embrace the 4IR:

i. *The IIoT*: machines and technologies collecting, sharing, and acting on data between themselves.

ii. *Big data*: the capture of data on everything and real-time analysis of that data by machines and systems.

iii. *Secure and reliable digital infrastructure*: a resilient network to link everything up.

5 Window of Opportunity for Emerging Economies in the 4IR

5.1 Emerging Market Economies of the World

The 4IR has the prospect of positively impacting not only developed economies but also developing economies across the globe irrespective of their level of development or location.

(Wood et al., 2018; Ayentimi & Burgess, 2019)

In the emerging market economy, the economy of a developing nation becomes more engaged with global markets as it grows. The emerging market economy is marked with pointers such as more integration with the global economy, increase in trade volume, more in-flow of Foreign Direct Investments (FDI), increased liquidity in local debt and equity markets, growth in domestic layouts of infrastructure projects, and implementation of modern policies in financial and regulatory institutions.

The major emerging economies of the world at present are Argentina, Brazil, Cambodia, Chile, China, Columbia, Egypt, Hungry, India, Indonesia, Iran, Malaysia, and Mexico. These are emerging countries as there has been substantial economic growth and the pace of economic growth is still high owing to the development of industrial and technological sectors. The growth though has been arrested by the pandemic situation since 2020. The emerging economies are more likely to embrace the 4IR to foster economic growth, as has already taken place in developed nations and is continuing at a great pace.

5.2 Leapfrogging Using Advanced Technologies

The cumulative benefits of the application of this new technological evolution – AI, robotics, genetics, 3D printing, nanotechnology, and biotechnology – can offer developing economies (i) increased productivity by scaling up agriculture and manufacturing production, (ii) new economic activities, (iii) new products and new markets, and (iv) revitalised employment growth in both the formal and informal sectors.

(Naudé 2017; Makridakis, 2017)

At present, the maximum economic benefit of the 4IR is with the handful of developed countries; however, the expansion, utilisation, and exploitation of the emerging technologies cannot be limited to the few. *The other countries that are the so-called latecomers in this field can accelerate their development by skipping some of the intermediary stages of industrialisation and leapfrogging into using more advanced technologies.*

The glaring example of this 'leapfrogging' phenomenon can be seen in most of the countries in the world which actually did not have landline coverage or only had partial coverage but which have all adopted the cellular technology so that mobiles are available even in the remotest of places on earth. Similar can be said and predicted about the 4IR. The developing countries, which hitherto have not been using the technologies extensively for manufacturing industries, can reach new levels of advancement by adopting new tools and technologies.

Proactive governments can certainly help to reduce the technological gaps by creating partnerships at both national and international levels, thus delivering a forum for gains in infrastructure. International organisations such as the International Trade Center, the World Bank Group, and the WEF can also play their role. The provision of vital software and hardware resources will supply a platform for the emerging nations to thrive in a sustainable manner. *While the developed world persists in rumbling along at a breakneck speed, it is crucial that the emerging nations are leapfrogging to the trajectory of development plotted by the 4IR.*

5.3 Absorption of 4IR Technologies by Emerging Economies

With the 4IR underway at an astonishing speed in developed countries, the emerging and developing nations must embrace it without wasting any time. If the current emerging economies want to seize the complete benefit of the 4IR, they will need to commence applying foundations to get involved sooner rather than later. Technology and education are two primary spots where the emerging nations could benefit from the 4IR, while macro- and microeconomic and social policies for growth are additional elements to pay regard to.

> The Southeast Asian countries have shifted their specialisation towards manufacturing, nurtured a domestic entrepreneurial class, and now host a multi-polar – Japan, Korea, China – regional industrial landscape where competition and diversification co-exist with specialisation in new paradigms, mostly electronics, automotive, and digital technologies.
>
> (Primi and Toselli, 2020)

The 4IR and Industry 4.0 can be windows of opportunity for developing and emerging economies but also raise red flags in terms of the main challenges that these changes pose to developing and emerging economies' firms, industrial systems, and policy approaches. Benefitting from them will not be automatic, as developing economies suffer from several gaps that hamper their ability to operate in a digital industrial landscape. However, with capable and forward-looking entrepreneurial states, developing economies could actually use the ongoing uncertain and fast-changing scenarios to fast-track their development.

A major novelty with respect to the past is that, as partnerships become more relevant for innovations owing to technological convergence, competition policies and standards to avoid monopolistic positions and excessive concentration are needed to maintain the space for bottom-up innovation. To do so, developing and emerging economies will need to manage complex policy agendas, ranging from skills development and infrastructure to standards, intellectual property, and taxation. Investing in strengthening domestic firms' capabilities and implementing policies to foster learning and capabilities accumulation in national innovation systems remain crucial building blocks of industrialisation strategies and of successful participation and upgrading in Global Value Chains (GVC), even in an Industry 4.0 landscape.

6 Impact of the 4IR on Emerging Economies

Technological breakthroughs such as big data and AI, demographic changes such as an ageing population and the shortage of a human workforce in several rapidly ageing economies, rapid urbanisation, and shifts in global economic power between developed and developing countries with a large working-age population are the key factors and driving force for the future of work. The outcome of all this is *societal transformation* on a global scale by influencing the incentives, regulations, and norms of economic life, bringing in changes to how we communicate, interact, learn, entertain ourselves, and relate to one another. Moreover, the rapid pace at which new technologies are being developed and executed is impacting human conscience, identities, communities, societies, and political structures.

As a result, our responsibilities to each other, opportunities for self-realisation, and our capabilities to impact the world positively are intricately tied to and formed by how we engage and interact with the technologies of the 4IR. *This revolution is not just happening to us – we are not its targets – rather, we bear the opportunity and obligation to provide it with form and meaning.* With these elemental changes which are underway, we have the opportunity to proactively shape the 4IR to be both inclusive and human-centred. This revolution is about more than technology; it is a chance to connect international communities, build durable economies, adjust and update governance prototypes, decrease material and social imbalances, and dedicate to value-based leadership of arising technologies. The 4IR is thus not a forecast of tomorrow but a catalyst for change. It is a fabrication for developing, diffusing, and handling technologies in patterns that enable a more empowering, cooperative, and tolerant basis for social and economic development around shared values of common interest, human satisfaction, and intergenerational stewardship.

There are three reasons why today's changes convey not a prolongation of the Third Industrial Revolution but instead the appearance of a Fourth Industrial

Revolution and a different one: momentum, area, and approaches. The pace of current breakthroughs has no documented precedent. When compared with earlier industrial revolutions, the 4IR is developing at an exponential instead of a linear rate. Moreover, it is disrupting almost every enterprise in every country. And the scope and profundity of these shifts indicate the change of entire systems of production, control, and administration.

The technologies that underpin the 4IR will have a significant influence on businesses. On the supply side, multiple industries are witnessing the introduction of new technologies that form unique methods of serving living necessities and greatly disrupt living industry value chains. It will enhance the grade, rate, or cost at which value is given. It will even lead to significant changes on the demand-side areas, increasing transparency, consumer attention, and new practices of consumer conduct (increasingly made upon entry to mobile networks and data), and push companies to adjust the way they develop, market, and deliver products and services.

Disrupting existing supply channels or the on-demand economy will help the evolution of technology-enabled platforms that incorporate both demand and supply elements. These technology outlets will create altogether new ways of consuming goods and services. This will reduce the hindrances for businesses and individuals to make wealth, varying the personal and professional backgrounds of workers. The business areas that the 4IR will most affect are customer expectations, product enhancement, joint innovation, and administrative processes.

New technologies and venues will increasingly allow citizens to engage with governments, express their thoughts, harmonise their measures, and even circumvent the control of public authorities. However, the governments will acquire new technological capabilities to improve their control over populations, based on pervasive surveillance systems and the power to manage digital infrastructure. But they will increasingly be forced to transform their existing approach to public engagement and policymaking.

The 4IR will profoundly affect the essence of national and international security, concerning both the likelihood and the nature of the conflict. The advances in technology will create the potential to reduce the scale or impact of violence, through the growth of new methods of protection, for example, or greater precision in targeting.

The 4IR may undoubtedly have the possibility to 'robotise' society but, as an addendum to the most reasonable components of human nature – imagination, compassion, stewardship – it can also raise humanity to new standards through a sense of collective destiny. Developing economies can thus seize the chance to shape the 4IR towards a tomorrow that reflects their shared plans and pursuits.

In light of the widespread acceptability and scope of the informal economy in developing nations, the transition from informal to gig labour represents less of a movement in the nature of the job than it does a shift in the manner in which the work is obtained. It has been suggested by the Brookings Institute that a shift towards the gig economy will result in a 'digitalization of informality' (Loo, 2017). Because of the 4IR, new options to formalise employment that had previously been labelled informal are being generated, as are new chances to incorporate developing best practices from the gig economy.

It will be necessary to completely restructure the industrial sector in order to keep up with this technological tsunami. Because of low labour costs in developing countries, the majority of them rely on employment outsourcing. Emerging countries, on the other hand, are beginning to see the tremendous potential they have, and they will make every effort to bring production back home in order to deliver more affordable and effective manufacturing through the use of smart technology. However, before they can reap the benefits of new technology, these emerging nations must first overcome a number of challenges. For these countries to begin reaping the benefits of the 4IR, there are a number of areas in which they must make advancements (Asghar et al., 2020).

Small states and emerging countries have the possibility to jump immediately into the 4IR without having to go through the previous three industrial revolutions. This necessitates governments giving high priority to the transition to the 4IR and creating a sense of urgency around it. This is already happening in some countries that are establishing Centres for the Fourth Industrial Revolution (World Economic Forum, 2020a); however, governments in small states and developing countries need to empower citizens to use emerging technologies for sustainable development in their own contexts (Cissé, 2018). According to Rudge (2019), '[f]or Small Island Developing States in particular, the Fourth Industrial Revolution could have a truly positive transformative effect – especially if we look at how these economies could join the Creative Industries Revolution. It's going to take something of a shift in thinking though'.

Developing nations and their governments were prevented from fully participating in the preceding three industrial revolutions owing to, among other things, a lack of infrastructure, skills, and experience. Countries are increasingly well positioned to take advantage of digital technology in the 4IR to make them move towards sustainable development and, in turn, to better the lives of their populations. Developing countries and small states must make it a priority to adopt 4IR technologies and scale up their implementation (Adhikari, 2020). The advent of the 4IR has resulted in a shift from the large computer revolution (Third Industrial Revolution) to the development of smart technologies such as AI, IoT, robotics, and data analytics (Philbeck and Davis, 2019).

The following are some of the difficulties that emerging countries face:

i. a general lack of understanding about the 4IR;
ii. a lack of a strategy for implementing the 4IR;
iii. a lack of collaboration between industry and academics;
iv. an absence of infrastructure;
v. a scarcity of expertise in the relevant fields.

Simultaneously, emerging economies such as South Africa, India, and China are relying on 4IR technologies to ensure their future development. UNESCO and the WEF have supported initiatives to educate nations about the benefits of adopting 4IR technologies for sustainable development and improvement in quality of life. In 2019, UNESCO hosted two conferences: 'Artificial Intelligence for Sustainable Development'[1] and the 'International Conference on Artificial Intelligence and Education, Planning Education in the AI Era: Lead the Leap'.[2] The 'Artificial Intelligence for Sustainable Development' symposium[3] was attended by more than 1,500 participants from 140 countries, including ministers of education and information and communication technology (ICT), other representatives from the Commonwealth Member States, and members of the private sector, academia, and international organisations. The overall aim of the conference was to explore the opportunities and threats linked to the use of AI in education. Specific topics included: how to ensure inclusive and equitable use of AI in education; how to leverage AI to enhance education and learning; how to promote skills development for jobs and life in the AI era; and how to safeguard transparent and auditable use of education data.[4] The second conference, which was 'Artificial Intelligence and Education: Planning Education in the AI Era: Lead the Leap',[5] was attended by around 500 international representatives from more than 100 Member States, United Nations agencies, academic institutions, civil society organisations, and the private sector; amongst these were fifty government ministers and deputy ministers.

The Director-General of UNESCO reiterates that:

> Promoting open-access AI tools that will encourage local innovation will be one of our priorities. To prepare future generations for the new landscape of work that AI is creating, it will also be necessary to rethink educational programmes, with an emphasis on science, technology, engineering and mathematics – but also giving a prominent place to the humanities and to competencies in philosophy and ethics. (Ally, 2020; Azoulay, 2018)

---

[1] https://en.unesco.org/themes/ict-education/ai-education-conference-2019.
[2] https://iite.unesco.org/theme/digital-literacy/.   [3] https://en.unesco.org/mlw/2019.
[4] https://unesdoc.unesco.org/ark:/48223/pf0000370308.
[5] https://unesdoc.unesco.org/ark:/48223/pf0000370967.

In an era when emerging countries are struggling with poverty and rising unemployment – for example, South Africa is experiencing riots as a result of job losses and the economic impact of COVID-19 – the 4IR and the promise of a digital economy have the potential to transform the fortunes of emerging nations such as India, Indonesia, and South Africa. Data and AI may be used to solve a variety of such challenges. Additional capacity-building initiatives are required to catapult the nations into the 4IR. There are more available jobs than skilled workers in the current environment.

Industry 4.0 is a phrase that is frequently used to characterise the evolving process of manufacturing and chain production management. As such, it is significant for industrialised countries that rely heavily on production. The majority of developing countries, including Bangladesh, Nigeria, India, Pakistan, the Philippines, and Vietnam, rely on manufacturing goods for export. Therefore, if these nations can improve their manufacturing and chain production management, their present rate of unit output would grow significantly, indicating that Industry 4.0 is crucial for these countries to progress.

Bangladesh is one of the fastest developing economies in South Asia. The country has been criticised for a lack of output, labour skills, and unit production when compared with other major producers of ready-made garments (RMG), such as Thailand, Vietnam, and Mexico. Additionally, Bangladesh is critiqued for a lack of female leadership, a lack of manufacturing infrastructure, a lack of technical application, and a lack of adaptation to industry development and availability, all of which are regarded as important issues for this developing country (Islam and Jantan, 2017). According to experts, a country that integrates and utilises technology in manufacturing may significantly expand its production ranges; so, Industry 4.0 is critical since it automates and exchanges data in manufacturing technologies (Lasi et al., 2014; Buhr, 2015; Berawi, 2018). As a result, it is critical for the country to raise its manufacturing efficiency in order to earn more foreign money.

7 Emerging Economies and Global Value Chains

7.1 Connotation of Global Value Chains

Global Value Chains (GVC) refer to international production sharing, a phenomenon where production is broken into activities and tasks carried out in different countries (Seric and Tong, 2019). In GVC, the full range of activities, such as design, production, marketing, distribution, and support to the final customers and the end-users, is divided amongst multiple firms and workers across geographical spaces to bring a product from its conception to its end use and beyond.

It is a large-scale, worldwide extension of the *division of labour* as popularised by Adam Smith. In his first sentence of *An Inquiry into the Nature and Causes of the Wealth of Nations* (1776), Smith foresaw the essence of industrialism by determining that division of labour represents a substantial increase in productivity. His famous example was the making of a pin:

> One man draws the wire; another straightens it; a third cuts it; a fourth points it; a fifth grinds it at the top for receiving the head; to make the head requires two or three distinct operations; to put it on is a peculiar business; to whiten the pins is another; it is even a trade by itself to put them into the paper; and the important business of making a pin is in this manner, divided into eighteen distinct operations, are all performed by distinct hands. (Kay, 2021)

In GVCs, the operations and activities are performed across national borders, instead of being confined to one particular place, and the products made are much more complex than a mere pin.

The 4IR has driven the GVCs across the continents. This development has largely been possible because of the transnational corporations (TNC) which have been continuously restructuring their businesses and reorganising or relocating their operations for reasons of competition, cost, and profits.

7.2 Methods of Adoption of GVCs by Emerging and Developing Countries

Most of the emerging economies suffer gaps that hamper their ability to embrace the 4IR and realise the potential of Industry 4.0. Developing economies tend to be specialised in producing and trading commodities, suffer from digital connectivity gaps, and, especially, have a limited knowledge base; on average, they invest little – much less than advanced countries – in research and development (R & D) and innovation. In addition, their private sector is more risk-averse and contributes little to national innovation efforts. Given this situation, their participation in GVCs will not activate learning processes per se, unless targeted policies are put in place.

A deeper look at the global trends reveals that few countries, and in practice only some specific areas within them, have been able to benefit from growing global interconnectedness (Primi and Toselli, 2020). Specifically, the challenge for emerging and developing economies is to upgrade into the high-end segment of GVCs. This is because merely joining the GVC does not guarantee upgrading (Lee and Malerba, 2017). An economy might be stuck in low-value activities without functional upgrading, causing the so-called middle-income trap (World Bank, 2010; Lee, 2013).

Therefore, the key challenge for emerging and developing economies is to find the 'right and dynamic' mode and ways of participation in GVC, with the long-term goal of building and upgrading their own 'local chains for value and knowledge creation' thereby leveraging a bigger piece of the pie from the global profit (Lee and Malerba, 2017). Actually, the objective which defines the strategy of entering into a determined value chain has a major impact on subsequent learning and development. Participation in the automotive value chain in Mexico was fuelled by the need to generate employment.

At the initial stage, the developing countries should decide on the specific value chains, giving all their wherewithal to this value chain, subsequently increasing domestic value-added by seeking separation and independence from the existing foreign-dominated GVC, and after that stage latecomer firms and economies might have to seek again more opening or integration once they have built their own local value chains. This dynamic sequence of 'in-out-in again' would generate more integration and participation in GVCs.

A paper using the trade in value-added data identifies different patterns of participation in GVCs. On the one hand, they identify a group of countries '*climbing the ladder*' in terms of increasing more proportionally the domestic value-added embodied in foreign exports than the foreign value-added embodied in domestic exports. On the other hand, they identify another group of countries '*deepening in assembly*' where an increase in foreign value-added embodied in domestic exports increases more proportionally than the domestic value-added embodied in foreign exports.

According to the evidence provided by Primi and Toselli (2020), China has been able to climb the ladder in three industries (textile, automotive, and electronics) by increasing more proportionally the domestic value-added embodied in foreign imports than the foreign value-added embodied in domestic exports. This contrasts with Mexico whose two main sectors – automotive and electronics – belong to the deepening-in-assembly group. Mexico faces in fact the middle-income trap risk and has not capitalised enough on its participation in GVCs.

As per the same paper by Primi and Toselli (2020), with the exception of China, few developing economies have been able to associate this upgrading and increased participation in global production networks with processes of home-grown branding and the creation of leading multinationals. In fact, most of the increased participation of developing economies in GVCs took place through increased absorption of foreign technology, capital, and knowledge, therefore resulting in processes of deepening-in-assembly functions, associated with little, if not absent, home-grown branding creation processes (as in the case of the automotive industry in Mexico and electronics in Vietnam).

7.3 The Role of Emerging Economies in GVCs

Emerging economies are playing significant and diverse roles in GVCs. In the last two decades, they were simultaneously exporters of intermediate and final manufactured goods (China, South Korea, Mexico) and primary products (Brazil, Russia, South Africa). The market growth has also led to shifting end markets in GVCs as more trade has occurred between the developing economies after the 2008–9 economic recession. China has been the focal point of both trends: it is the world's largest importer of many raw materials thereby contributing to the primary products export boom.[6]

Gary Gereffi, in his working paper titled 'Global Value Chains, Development and Emerging Economies' (2015), cites three aspects of GVCs: (i) promoting growth and upgrading in export-oriented GVCs, (ii) leveraging local knowledge to add value in resource-based GVCs, and (iii) the role of public–private partnerships to narrow the human capital gap.

i. Promoting growth and upgrading in export-oriented GVCs
Central America is considered one of the world's leading speciality coffee producers. Countries in this region such as Guatemala, Honduras, Nicaragua, and Panama produce coffee of a special grade. Most of the speciality coffee comes from small producers and the challenge has been to provide them with a sustainable niche in the speciality coffee GVC. However, they are faced with the difficulty that the Coffee Valve Chain is dominated by a few large exporters, along with roasters who are located near the final consumers in North America, Europe, and East Asia (Gereffi, 2015). Obstacles like high infrastructure needs, high cost of inputs, and inadequate short-term financing are faced by the smallholders. *That can be overcome by the creation of strong national or regional coffee associations, which could provide a major boost to export producers in Central America thus making the small producers able to command high prices for their speciality coffee, bringing economic upgrading of smallholder farmers of this region.*

Similarly, another example is Brazil and Mexico, which have benefitted from automobile GVCs wherein the local suppliers are fully integrated with the TNCs. The automotive GVC has created more jobs in Mexico but has higher skill levels and technological capabilities in Brazil (Gereffi, 2015).

ii. Leveraging local knowledge to add value in resource-based GVCs
The example cited by Gereffi is Uruguay, where cows outnumber people by four to one and beef is the leading export. However, the global beef industry

---

[6] www.unido.org.

is extremely vulnerable to health and food safety problems. In 2000, a multi-year ban on its export to the USA, EU, Chile, South Korea, and Israel was imposed on Uruguay for a foot and mouth disease outbreak in cows. Uruguay then embarked upon the development of a sophisticated bovine traceability system which would allow the country to quickly and efficiently track the source of and contain potential problems and maintain consumer and regulatory confidence in their products in the developed world. The Livestock Traceability System was developed through a collaborative multi-stakeholder initiative bringing together producers, local governments, transport personnel, the private sector, IT companies, and the central government. Today this is the only system in the world with real-time monitoring of 100 per cent of the national cattle herd. A chip implanted in each cow's ear at birth allows the system to keep centralised and accurate information regarding the animal from birth through to sales and distribution points.

Uruguay has a great opportunity to export its knowledge and experiences to other countries that face similar issues. Many nations have started this system. This means Uruguay can participate in different segments of the Cattle Value Chain. Now the country has the potential to export advanced services in not only the beef industry but the broader livestock sector as well.

iii. The role of public–private partnerships to narrow the human capital gap
National finishing schools represent a promising tool to narrow the gap between the human capital needs of GVCs and the skills supplied by national education systems. The Finishing School Model has been tested in India. These schools help recent graduates and workers develop high-demand skills, making them more employable. In turn, by increasing workforce employability, finishing schools can help a country improve its position in the value chain. In India, the most effective finishing schools are those that collaborated with companies to identify the desired skill set and match training to the gaps. In the global service industry, these skills often include IT skills, English abilities, and soft skills such as relational skills, confidence, and presentation skills

Public–private partnerships are central to creating effective financing and governance mechanisms to support finishing school programmes. Both private and government institutions are playing their roles in this regard. The Finishing School Model recognises the role of all stakeholders – the State, academia, and industry – in shaping the capabilities of the labour pool towards delivering information technology and business process outsourcing services.

8 How Is India Adopting the 4IR to Build Economic Value?

8.1 Initiatives Taken by Government to Adopt Industry 4.0

India is the second-largest emerging economy after China. In its drive to imbibe 4IR and Industry 4.0, the Government of India has taken several initiatives in recent times to provide the necessary infrastructure within the country to facilitate the adoption of 4IR. The Government of India, through its unique initiatives like Digital India, Startup India, and Make in India, is bolstering the opportunities for 4IR and green entrepreneurs.

Launched in July 2015, *Digital India* is a flagship programme of the Government of India with a vision to transform India into a digitally empowered society and knowledge economy.[7] The programme is centred on three key vision areas: (i) digital infrastructure as a core utility to every citizen, (ii) governance and services on demand, and (iii) digital empowerment of citizens. The programme thus is moving forward to ensure the government's services are made available to citizens by improved online infrastructure and by increasing internet connectivity, thus making the country digitally empowered.

Launched in August 2015, the *Startup India* initiative is a flagship initiative that aims to build a strong ecosystem for nurturing innovations and start-ups in the country, which will drive sustainable economic growth and generate large-scale employment opportunities. An action plan was announced later, touching on areas such as funding support and incentives, industry–academia partnership, and incubation.[8]

Launched in September 2014, the *Make in India* initiative is a part of a wider set of nation-building initiatives devised to transform India into a global design and manufacturing hub.[9] The aim has been to encourage companies to develop, manufacture, and assemble products made in India and to incentivise dedicated investment in manufacturing (BloombergQuint, n.d.).

India still lags behind its global peers in adoption of the 4IR. Over the past few years, owing to several policy initiatives by the State, India has been able to improve its ranking in several global indices. India is able to position itself as one of the countries with a focus on innovation and competitiveness. The most important step in this direction was the setting up of the Centre for the 4IR in India. The world recognition of India's potential is apparent as the WEF has partnered with the Government of India to set up this centre in India. The initial focus of the centre will be on drones, AI, and blockchain technology. The National Institution for Transforming India (NITI) Aayog, business leaders,

---

[7] https://digitalindia.gov.in. [8] www.startupindia.gov.in. [9] www.makeinindia.com.

start-ups, and academia will be part of this project of the WEF. The centre in India is fourth in the world after San Francisco, Tokyo, and Beijing.

India's Global Innovation Index ranking has drastically improved over the years. In September 2021, India stood 46th in the Global Innovation Index prepared by the World Intellectual Property Organisation. India continues to lead the world in the ICT in services export indicator (1st) and holds top ranks in other indicators, such as domestic industry diversification (12th) and graduates in science and engineering (12th). The improvement in the ranking has been due to immense knowledge capital, a vibrant start-up ecosystem, and the work done by the public and private research organisations.

> The Centre for the Fourth Industrial Revolution India has been developed in partnership with the Government of India through the National Institution for Transforming India (NITI) Aayog. Located in Mumbai, the centre serves as a trusted space where local and foreign policy-makers, business executives, technology experts and other key stakeholders exchange insights on the latest technological trends and applications and help shape the future of the Fourth Industrial Revolution. (World Economic Forum, 2020b)

The Government of India has set an ambitious target of increasing the contribution of manufacturing output to 25 per cent of Gross Domestic Product (GDP) by 2025, from 16 per cent currently (Sage Metals, 2019). The IoT, being one of the most important aspects of Industry 4.0 for India, is expected to capture close to a 20 per cent share in the global IoT market in the next five years (Kalaria, 2019). According to India Brand Equity Foundation (IBEF), a trust established by the Government of India, the IoT market in India is projected to grow at a Compound Annual Growth Rate (CAGR) of more than 28 per cent during 2015–2020.

The Government of India has taken on initiatives such as the *Green Energy Corridor Project*, which aims at synchronising electricity produced from renewable sources such as solar and wind with conventional power stations in the grid (Thomas, 2022). The Indian government has created green energy corridors to bring in more renewable energies to make smart grids that will support the variable input of renewable energies and create storage. India has committed over US$ 1 billion to this initiative and has started projects in many states, such as Andhra Pradesh, Rajasthan, Tamil Nadu, Gujarat, and Himachal Pradesh.

India's first *smart factory*, moving from automation to autonomy, where machines speak with each other, is being set up in Bengaluru. It is making progress at the Indian Institute of Science's (IISc) Centre for Product Design and Manufacturing (CPDM) with an investment from the Boeing Company. A smart factory, armed with data exchange in manufacturing and the IoT, is the future and experts are calling it Industry 4.0. Reports peg the smart factory industry to touch US$ 215 billion by 2025 and all major economies are likely to accept it.

8.2 The Role of the Confederation of Indian Industry in Smart Manufacturing

The Confederation of Indian Industry (CII) works to create and sustain an environment conducive to the development of India, partnering with industry, government, and civil society, through advisory and consultative processes.[10] The CII has been playing a leadership role in the advent of 4IR in the country. CII Smart Manufacturing Council was created in April 2017, comprising industry experts from around fifty companies to focus on the agenda of *smart manufacturing in the Indian context*. This Council has undertaken significant work to promote the creation of an enabling ecosystem that promotes the adoption of smart manufacturing at various levels – macro (ecosystem), meso (institutions), and micro (firm).

In April 2018, CII worked with the Department of Heavy Industry, Government of India, to formulate a smart manufacturing blueprint that identified key interventions required by various nodal ministries towards fostering the adoption of smart manufacturing in India. On 26 October 2018, CII launched an online portal that showcased detailed case studies of around thirty companies that had deployed smart manufacturing in India.[11] The portal outlines the implementation journeys, with details on the challenges faced before implementation, an overview of Industry 4.0 solutions, and benefits reaped post-deployment.

CII also organised an International Learning Mission to Germany from 23 to 26 April 2018 on the fringes of Hannover Messe to help the industry understand the contours of transformation in the manufacturing sector and witness smart manufacturing in action. CII has been actively advocating the creation of a government–industry co-led Platform on Industry 4.0 in India (similar to Platform Industries 4.0, Germany), to not only help synergise activities taken up by various stakeholders but also foster the adoption of next-generation practices in mission mode. The platform's focus will include norms and standards, the security and legal framework for Industry 4.0, research and innovation, and skills development. It will encourage and help high-tech start-ups to expand in-house development of IoT and big data capabilities as key enablers of Industry 4.0.

---

[10] www.cii.in/About_Us.aspx?enc=ns9fJzmNKJnsoQCyKqUmaQ==.　　[11] www.ciismart.in.

8.3 Enablers to Actualise India's Sustainable Transformation to the 4IR

India is living all industrial revolutions at the same time. It is difficult to imagine but true. It has a vast number of small factories that use basic technology – the First Industrial Revolution. It has world-class companies in steel, automobiles, and petrochemicals – the Second Industrial Revolution. It is a global leader in software, and telecommunications has been the backbone of its recent growth – the Third Industrial Revolution. And it has to prepare for automation and digitalisation, the harbingers of the Fourth Industrial Revolution. The enablers that can realise India's aim of embracing the 4IR and Industry 4.0 positively are:

i.   Creation of an enabling ecosystem through incubators and accelerators to develop and scale up innovations in 'Future Now' Cleantech sectors like clean energy, climate-smart agriculture, circular economy, green buildings, and e-mobility, critical in the Indian context to achieving transformative goals. Incubators, accelerators, and innovation labs provide the necessary technical and financial support across various lifecycle stages of a start-up by creating a collaborative and mentoring platform. For instance, Infuse is a venture catalyst and an exemplary first-of-its-kind partnership between government, academia, and corporate to pool-in technology, business, market, and policy expertise to scale up Cleantech business in India (Vikas, 2018).

ii. Proactive initiatives and policies to build on the positive aspects of the new industrial revolution and prevent further widening of the inequality gap.

iii. Access to finance commensurate with the maturity of the business model and the beginning stage of the start-up lifecycle is extremely important to scale up innovations. While government-led initiatives like Start-Up Sangam will play a key role in crowding-in capital, private sector participation through grants, seed funding, equity capital, and mainstream debt is necessary to scale up innovations. Corporates will have a key role in championing this ongoing movement, leveraging the ART model (alliances, relationships enabled through technology). Globally, there are examples of corporates like Saint-Gobain supporting Greentown Labs, the largest Cleantech start-up incubator in the United States, Wells Fargo Innovation Incubator aimed towards reducing the energy impact of commercial buildings, and Shell Foundation Incubator, focussing efforts on identifying potential game-changers aimed at helping low-income customers to gain access to electricity (Vikas, 2018).

India has to invest in the enablers and the drivers and synergise India's soft-power skillset, gain government support, and foster a sense of urgency in private organisations and entities to leapfrog into the 4IR.

9 How Is China Adopting the 4IR to Build Economic Value?

China was one of the most significant victims of the First and Second Industrial Revolutions, which were spurred by the invention of the steam engine and the invention of electricity, respectively. After falling victim to the Manchus, as had happened previously to the Mongolian hunters who had invaded and captured the heart of China, the Qing Dynasty was engulfed in a series of wars with 'industrialised' nations from Europe and Japan. Although the country's misfortunes persisted after the collapse of the final dynasty in the early twentieth century, wars, famines, and political upheaval characterised the country's history until the conclusion of the Cultural Revolution in the late 1970s. After more than a century of seclusion, the Chinese people did not experience the Second Industrial Revolution until the early 1980s, when they opted to integrate into the global economy for the first time. As a result of China's entry into the modern industrialised world at the same time as the Third Industrial Revolution, it is often considered to be the most momentous event in human history since the beginning of the First Industrial Revolution.

Since the early 1980s, China has been able to accomplish in one generation what would have taken five or more generations in the West. The country has already surpassed the United States as the world's second-biggest economy, and given the recent retreat of major Western countries from globalisation, its worldwide impact is only expected to rise in the future.

This time around, at the outset of the 4IR, China is in a far better position than it has been in the past to exploit the opportunities presented by industrial change. Indeed, it may be better positioned than any other major economy to benefit from the shift that is about to take place.

One of the most significant changes in the global development landscape since the 1990s has been the steady and rapid ascent of China as a worldwide power in the shape of an emerging market, which has occurred since the 1990s. At a time when digital technologies and the 4IR are developing and increasing their potential influence, China's progress is rewriting the global rules of the game. Furthermore, this has a significant influence on economic potential in new and emerging markets. It is therefore critical for emerging and developing economies to identify the appropriate and dynamic mode of cooperation in GVCs, with the long-term aim of fostering and upgrading their own local chains for value and knowledge creation, and by doing so utilising a larger share of the global profit pie in the long run (Lee et al., 2018). As the global order shifts and some emerging economies begin to accumulate know-how and capabilities, advanced countries have begun to feel the pressure of losing their industrial and technological leadership. As a result, advanced countries have begun to shift their attitudes towards investment, trade, and delocalisation of production.

Researchers have discovered that China has a highly centralised innovation system with numerous mission-oriented policy sub-systems, the most important of which are knowledge and innovation, defence-related innovation, regional development, and social networking. The authors also note that the science and technology agency service system is highly centralised. China is now attempting to widen its industrial base, increase its knowledge absorption capacity, and shift its focus to high-tech and higher-value-added enterprises, among other things. In comparison to Germany's Industry 4.0, the vision of Made in China 2025 is more comprehensive in scope and involves a more organised implementation phase, according to the Chinese government. Its primary objective is to elevate China from the status of a manufacturing country to that of a manufacturing powerhouse on a global scale. Among the five major projects under the Made in China banner are the establishment of manufacturing innovation centres, the development of smart manufacturing technologies, the strengthening of manufacturing bases, the development of green manufacturing technologies, and the development of high-end equipment innovation technologies.

Traditionally known as the world's low-wage manufacturer, the Chinese economy is now seeking to make full use of automation and efficiency-improving innovation. But can the world's most populous nation accept a system that threatens to significantly decrease the labour market? It is obvious that China has been able to build a far more stable labour market.

According to PwC:

> As China becomes more innovative and less imitative, there will also be an ever-growing demand for manufacturing technologies such as robots, drones, and autonomous vehicles. Chinese industrial employment is therefore likely to shift from lower value, labour-intensive production to higher-value roles, including those involved in the manufacture of AI-enabled equipment for export, as well as to meet rising domestic demand. (Middleton, 2018)

The world is currently undergoing the 4IR, which is an era in which technological advancements are having an enormous influence on the way people live their lives. In every facet of our life, as well as every business, including the financial markets, it has an influence. It's defining what it means to be human in the information age, according to Zvika Krieger, the WEF's head of Technology Policy.

Leaders of the WEF stated at the 2019 World Economic Forum's Annual Meeting of the New Champions, also known as the 2019 Summer Davos Forum, held in Dalian, northeast China's Liaoning province, that China has played a leading role in technological innovation and intellectual property protection during the 4IR and has the potential to continue to do so in the years to come (Yang, 2019). China has unquestionably established itself as a technological powerhouse and global leader in recent years. It's almost impossible to find a technology on the global scene where China is not the leader.

In addition to economic growth, the Chinese government's expenditure on R & D is having a significant influence on the technical ecosystem of the country and the rest of the world, allowing it to maintain its leading position. As China transfers and upgrades its manufacturing industry via innovation, its expenditure on R & D is second only to the United States and is surpassing that of Japan.

10 Emerging Countries to Turn Youth and Women into Assets for the 4IR

The introduction of the 4IR provides businesses throughout the world with a chance to influence youth workforce development and employment in general. Business leaders and the governments in emerging and developing countries face four difficulties as they continue to assess the broad influence they wish to have on young workforce development and employment and as individual organisations begin to consider the return they may expect from their investments in this area:

i. *Reframe the 4IR as a once-in-a-lifetime opportunity to be welcomed rather than a problem to be solved.* While the 4IR is sometimes characterised as a challenge, it actually presents an enormous opportunity. With rapidly increasing technology and shifting workplace developments, there is an opportunity to rethink how skills are associated with employment, how potential workers may show these talents, and how to establish new and more inclusive pipelines for the world's most marginalised youth. The business community can rebrand itself as an agent of change, generating employment and opportunity for the youth, our workplaces, and our globe. By capitalising on these 4IR possibilities, businesses can assist youth in finding work and improve individual economic mobility.

ii. *Investment and strategic planning.* Investments and strategic planning are necessary; funds and programmes alone will not be sufficient to employ the world's youngsters. Businesses, school systems, workforce development programmes, governments, communities, parents, and youth all have views, skills, solutions, roles, and the potential to collaborate in an integrated and forward-thinking manner in this 4IR period. By addressing core causes and collaborating on a shared future vision with the help of technologies, these disparate stakeholders can address not only programmatic requirements but also systemic barriers.

iii. *Lift underprivileged youth.* In the business community, there is room to enhance how best practices are planned, built and iterated upon, prototyped, and communicated. This includes how and where models are scaled, as well as chances to collaborate on a variety of learning and skill platforms. The business community, working together and via its influence, may position itself as the 'rising tide' that lifts youth, particularly those from underprivileged communities, into the world of employment.

iv. *Opportunities for women.* Giving opportunities to marginalised youth, especially those who have historically been difficult to reach, with a particular focus on women and girls.

It is not enough to reach youth through established networks or the most easily available channels. Rather than following traditional channels, the corporate community and the state governments should seek out and help the most difficult to reach youngsters who are the most disadvantaged and in most need of the technologies and opportunities that the 4IR can provide. Collaborators in the ecosystem are familiar with them, have worked with them, and can assist in bridging the gap so that their skills may be leveraged for the benefit of the whole ecosystem. As a result of these four challenges, and in consideration of the following recommendations, the business sector should explore how it might effectively harness its current resources and experience to help youth in the 4IR.

11 Risks and Challenges of Adoption of the 4IR for Emerging Economies

The World Economic Forum in Davos, Switzerland in 2019 explored the new global concerns that have emerged in the age of globalisation (Schwab, 2019). The executive chair expressed concern about three technology-related challenges created by the 4IR to domestic policies and international cooperation, including (1) urgent ecological constraints, (2) multipolarity of international action, and (3) rising inequality of socio-economic outcomes.

There are some challenges associated with the 4IR for growing economies, such as its potential to raise inequality in the world as the spread of machines boosts markets and disrupts labour markets. Imbalance symbolises the most prominent societal apprehension associated with the 4IR. The major challenges to be faced by emerging countries in embracing the 4IR are:

i. *Skills for the use of new technologies.* 4IR technologies and their applications often require specialist skills, beyond basic digital literacy. In an index of ten global cities' readiness to implement new technologies and current initiatives, Singapore came first but, according to research by PwC Russia, only 42 per cent of its residents surveyed felt ready to use them (Abdoola, 2019). To harness 4IR technologies for environmental sustainability in emerging nations, digital and 4IR awareness and skills need to be taught from an early age, and tailored higher education curriculums are required to equip school leavers and graduates with practical tools for work. Alongside this, older generations should not be left behind.

ii. *Low-skill, low-pay/high-skill, high-pay dichotomy of the workers.* One of the biggest beneficiaries of innovation tends to be the providers of intellectual and physical assets, the developers, shareholders, and investors, which explains the growing gap between those dependent on capital and those dependent on labour. As industrialisation replacements for labour across the whole economy, the net displacement of workers by machines might worsen the gap between returns to capital and returns to labour (Joseph and Nanjunga, 2020). With this trajectory, it is also likely that in the future, skill, more than capital, will represent the essential aspect of production. This will give rise to a job market increasingly segregated into low-skill, low-pay and high-skill, high-pay components, which in turn will lead to an escalation of social tensions.

iii. *Jobs and inequality.* The search for a better livelihood remains a driver of rapid urbanisation but the world of work is changing and increased automation is inevitable as technology use rises. Governments need to ensure that the opportunities and benefits of the 4IR are widely shared within and between cities and rural areas, and that the vulnerable and marginalised are not left further behind. This is particularly true in low- and middle-income countries where unemployment is high, especially for the youth. Reforms should focus on restructuring economies for a new, sustainable 4IR age, retraining those whose jobs become automated and re-evaluating the tax system and social protection schemes if there are fewer jobs available. Not doing so could exacerbate the negative environmental effects of inefficient resources and land use brought on by economic inequality.

iv. *Increased rural–urban migration.* Efficiency and competitiveness gains from 4IR deployment may attract more people to cities for economic opportunities, placing the urban environment under greater pressure and posing a risk to rural areas that are behind in development. Measures to mitigate negative effects involve ensuring adequate urban and infrastructure plans. For example, central government support for smarter villages helps to ensure openings for business and provides those living in villages and rural areas with fast digital access, in turn lessening the need to travel or move to urban areas.

v. *Energy intensity of 4IR technologies.* 4IR technologies can help to increase energy efficiency but their underlying use of energy is a cause for concern (e.g. the power required for blockchain and autonomous vehicles if they run on fossil-fuel-based energy). Government-led standards and incentives are needed to limit and, over time, reduce energy consumption from devices, sensors, and appliances and to promote renewable energy sources.

vi. *Effects on individuality.* The 4IR will transform not only what we do but even who we are. It will impact our individuality and all the subjects associated with it: our sense of privacy, our ideas of ownership, our consumption practices, the time we commit to working and relaxation, and how we grow our careers, develop our skills, meet people, and nurture affinities. In addition, low job creation, income unevenness, poor quality jobs, the gender pay gap, and the digital divide are some of the associated challenges that developing economies face for inclusive growth in the 4IR.

Cited above are the potential negative consequences and risks that may result from the use of technology unless corrective actions are taken. Besides these, the 4IR involves a tangle of interests that are potentially at odds with one another among other important stakeholders. Issues such as economic efficiency, sustainability, socio-economic development, ecological constraints, multipolarity of international action, and rising inequality of socio-economic outcomes among countries are a few of the risks and challenges which emerging and developing nations need to handle with care and balance in order to guarantee that new digital transformation does not create harmful effects in the spheres of international relations, varied sectors, and individuals' lives.

12 Mitigation of Risks

On the other side, when researchers and leaders examine the benefits of technological advancements, particularly the breakthroughs that have occurred during the 4IR, it becomes clear that, while these technologies have their own drawbacks and potential risks, they have or will soon become an integral part of humanity and will have a significant impact on human society as a whole.

Which way the balance will tilt, for good or bad, depends upon a plethora of tangible and intangible factors. However, history shows that humanity has emerged from each industrial revolution better technologically equipped, more scientifically advanced, and able to take future challenges in its stride.

To handle the apprehensions associated with the 4IR, diverse actions bolstering policy and the institutional ecosystem must be taken. Some of them are:

i. *Universal labour guarantee*: the emerging nations should commit to delivering a universal labour assurance that shields fundamental workers' rights, acceptable living pay, limits on hours of labour, and secure and healthy workplaces in their respective nations.

ii. *Lifelong education*: deliver a universal entitlement to lifelong learning that allows people to develop skills and to reskill and upskill.

iii. *Acquisition to sustain work shifts*: investment in the organisations, policies, and methods that will help people to select work shifts as per their convenience.

iv. *Plans for gender equality*: amplify women's voices and leadership, eradicate violence and harassment at work, and enforce pay transparency guidelines to attain gender equality.

v. *Social protection*: guaranteed social protection from birth to old age that helps people's requirements over the lifecycle should be provided.

vi. *Governance for digital platforms*: a national-level governance strategy for digital labour forums should be installed to protect the minimum rights of workers.

vii. *Sustainable work*: inducements are needed to encourage investment in key areas for proper and endurable work – the areas of environmental enterprise, rural economy, and small and medium corporations.

viii. *Human-centric business and economic model*: distributional proportions of growth, the significance of unpaid work performed for the benefit of households and neighbourhoods, and the externalities of economic activity, such as environmental degradation, should be taken into account for a human-centric business and economic model.

ix. *Data security*: necessary to maintain privacy, intellectual property rights, and related dimensions, to guarantee trustworthiness to transfer, process, and hoard the data that forms the basis of the 4IR.

x. *Tax evasion*: reconsidering fiscal policy becomes an unavoidable element; as products become virtual and services move online and are supplied remotely, there must be a peripheral check on tax evasion.

13 Can the 4IR Be a Sustainable Revolution?

Only a few emerging nations have the foundations and wherewithal for greater 4IR technology adoption, including ICT infrastructure and skilled workers, to embrace the 4IR in congruence with the Sustainable Development Goals 2030 as mandated by the United Nations. Many emerging and developing nations are struggling as they do not have adequate resources, the required ICT and related infrastructure, or the political will and correct government policies to align the adoption of 4IR technologies coherently and in unison with sustainable development.

The adoption of technologies along with meeting the SDGs will need different steps, new ways of working, and tailored solutions if the emerging nations are to leapfrog twentieth-century patterns of growth and development and meet overarching SDGs (UN, 2015). Partnerships and a spirit of collaboration across many stakeholders will define new governance models for the 4IR and will be necessary to ensure it is a sustainable revolution.

A 2019 UNESCO report titled 'Meeting commitments: are countries on track to achieve SDG4?' indicates that not only is the world far behind in meeting the 2030 educational sustainability goals but the ability to accurately address the dilemma is exacerbated by an inability to collect the necessary data (UNESCO, 2019). Inclusive economies and social development, individual and collective security and peace, and environmental sustainability constitute the foundational aims of the UN 2030 SDGs agenda (Habanik et al., 2019; Rosa, 2017; UN, 2015). As noted by Pollitzer (2019), 'the big transformational promise of 4IR is in cyberphysical systems that will merge different digital technologies and integrate them within the physical, digital, and biological spheres. This will produce deep and systemic societal changes at a larger scale and a more rapid rate than previously seen'.

13.1 Minimising Risks while Embracing the 4IR

Outlined below are non-exhaustive and broad recommendations to speed up innovation, minimise environmental risks, and increase the positive environmental impact of 4IR technologies for the emerging and developing nations:

(i) *Development strategies for the 4IR*: to build on 3IR-based strategies, identify quick-wins that demonstrate environmental value and applicability, and also enable planning delivery of further 4IR projects. Strategies need to be clear, tailored to urban and rural contexts, and integrated with a nationwide strategy, which engages with, and enjoys the support of, the private sector and citizens.

(ii) *National government ambitions and pragmatism*: to nurture and pursue innovation and context-specific 4IR applications. The State needs to show leadership and a willingness to act on the agenda for change, balancing visionary ambitions with pragmatism on risks and costs.

(iii) *Policy and regulatory environment*: to enable scaling of 4IR technologies and ensure these are developed and applied in a way that takes into account climate and the environment, business incentives and citizens' needs. Governments need to set transparent, adaptable, and enforceable policies, regulations, and standards.

(iv) *Innovative finance mechanisms*: to align the incentives as well as the risks of private-sector delivery of national-level 4IR projects and support early-stage commercialisation. National governments need to provide innovative PPP solutions, blended and risk finance, e.g. challenge funds and viability gap funding, to enable financing for the public good and technology development.

(v) *Information and engagement platforms*: to ensure collection, sharing, and public availability of data, nations need to lead in setting up platforms for collaboration as exemplified by subnational Open Government Partnership members or the Smart Hong Kong plan.

(vi) *Skills and retraining*: to build digital awareness (and use) among citizens, as well as to counter the negative effects of automation on jobs. National governments must promote new 4IR skills and retraining with a sustainability lens.

(vii) *Leadership on responsible business*: to ensure the 4IR is a sustainable revolution, the private sector, in alliance with governments, needs to take the lead on improving its own operations by embedding sustainability principles into 4IR technology design and investment decisions. Firms are key parts of the nation's economy and affect the environment locally and internationally via supply chains, often in emerging markets.

(viii) *Urban innovation pilots*: to solve the problems that matter for emerging cities, start-ups and big tech firms ought to invest in continued innovation, as well as devising pilots for specific cities to develop truly 'smart' sustainable solutions.

(ix) *Co-creation and collaboration*: to reach agreement and formulate the necessary governance for setting standards, sharing data, and other areas of 4IR engagement. Locally, the private sector needs to collaborate broadly with local government entities, utilities, and citizens.

(x) *Innovation ecosystems*: to capitalise on the creative energy already found in many cities, towns, and districts and develop local solutions. Businesses and investors can play a big role in the creation of city-based innovation hubs, incubators, and accelerators, supporting them to foster technology in the public interest, including those with environmental applications (Parsa, 2018).

(xi) *Educational partnerships*: to ensure vocational and university graduates are ready to enter the job market with practical tools integrating digital and sustainability. Academia, governments, and the private sector could partner in education for the 4IR.

(xii) *Community participation*: to ensure citizens benefit from the 4IR and that smart city designs are human-centred. Civil society groups and citizens should actively take part in local and national discussions on the form and direction of urban development in the 4IR.

13.2 Use of Artificial Intelligence for Sustainable Development

Artificial intelligence is rapidly opening up a new frontier in the fields of business, corporate practices, and governmental policy. The intelligence of machines and robotics with deep learning capabilities have created profound disrupting and enabling impacts on business, governments, and society. They are also influencing the larger trends in global sustainability (Goralskia and Tan, 2020). The AI Group of Experts at the OECD define an AI system as 'a machine-based system that can, for a given set of human-defined objectives, make predictions, recommendations or decisions influencing real or virtual environments' (Vincent-Lancrin and van der Vlies, 2020).

Artificial intelligence has the potential to: improve the welfare of people; contribute to positive, sustainable global economic activity; increase innovation and productivity; and help with responses to key global challenges, such as climate change, health crises, resource scarcity, and discrimination (OECD, 2019a).

Artificial intelligence holds significant potential to advance the agenda towards meeting sustainable development. AI can also be leveraged for social good and, to meet the United Nations SDGs in areas such as education, health, transport, agriculture, and sustainable cities, among others, many public and private organisations, including the World Bank, a number of United Nations agencies, and the OECD, are working to leverage AI to help advance the SDGs (OECD, 2019b).

As Vincent-Lancrin and van der Vlies (2020) argue, 'AI may particularly help achieve some of the global educational targets identified by the international community in SDG4: Ensure inclusive and equitable quality education and promote life-long learning opportunities for all'.

Goncharov (2020) lists the main benefits of the implementation of AI as:

- automation and widespread cost reduction;
- the emergence of autonomous transport and robotization;
- optimization of logistics processes and supply chains;
- optimization of energy and transport networks;
- development of sensor networks and monitoring of agriculture;
- development of information services and a distributed economy;
- development of personalized medicine, clinical practices and infrastructure for distributed and secure access to medical data;
- the emergence of personal educational trajectories and the development of social engineering;
- creation of autonomous weapons systems.

But the real question that arises is: how safe is it to depend on AI for your day-to-day work? The scientific field of AI – which encompasses a wide range of concepts and paradigms, data processing methods, semantic approaches, and technologies – is now the most sophisticated and promising area. Furthermore, algorithmic methods for developing intelligent systems based on formal-logical models, in a broad sense, represent the creation of syntactic structures that do not convey information about the content and meaning of data; as a result, systems based on these models can hardly be described as intelligent systems.

The United States is a global leader in AI. Many companies, such as Google, Amazon, Facebook, IBM, and dozens of start-ups, do substantial studies into the latest breakthroughs in this field. In 2018, the United States launched a $2 billion initiative to create the next generation of AI technologies with the objective of 'transforming computers from specialised tools into problem-solving partners'. At the same time, China is attempting to surpass the United States as the world leader in AI by 2030. China budgeted US$ 1.6 billion for development in 2017, and investments totalled US$ 4.9 billion in 2017, making it the world's largest investor in this sphere.

Despite the fact that the United States and China are the main participants, the development of AI is a worldwide phenomenon. The sector is growing at a rapid pace in both Israel and the United Kingdom. The promotion of innovation in the field of AI is also a major priority for governments in Japan, South Korea, and Russia. Countries that are able to create and implement advances in the field of AI will have excellent potential for economic growth as well as for boosting national security. Conversely, countries that continue to rely excessively on outdated infrastructure and economic models will find it difficult to sustain their competitiveness in the global marketplace.

Artificial Intelligence was formerly considered a science fiction concept but it is currently considered to be one of the most promising and fast advancing technologies available. AI systems with limited or 'weak' capabilities are now widely utilised in a variety of fields, ranging from mobile phones and domestic electronics to military equipment. At the moment, the creation of 'strong' AI, capable of making educated management decisions, is high on the priority list. According to experts, the potential of developing such a technology calls into question not just the present system of global labour division but the current world order and international security system as well.

14 Education and the 4IR

Education 4.0 is about aligning education systems through the use of 4IR technologies, to personalise learning and provide flexible learning opportunities for all citizens, regardless of location and status (Ally, 2019; Ally & Wark, 2019, September and November). Instead of needing learners to attend a physical site to study, the usage of online learning or e-learning enables learner-centred education to take place anywhere and at any time. Certain societal sectors, such as banking, e-commerce, business, government, manufacturing, and health, are leveraging 4IR technology to expand and deliver excellent services to residents. There is a sense of urgency in the education industry to leverage these technologies to deliver flexible education and personalised learning for long-term growth and achievement of the SDGs.

According to Vincent-Lancrin and van der Vlies (2020), in terms of instruction, AI's biggest promise lies in the personalisation of learning and learning materials; personalised learning is an educational approach aimed at customising learning based on students' individual needs and strengths; AI applications can identify pedagogical materials and approaches adapted to the level of individual students, and make predictions, recommendations, and decisions about the next steps in the learning process, based on data from individual students. According to Rubin and Brown (2019), there is a strong and vociferous consensus across all stakeholders today that our educational paradigm is not adequately educating kids for today, let alone for the challenges and possibilities of the future. They argue that a completely different strategy is required to bridge the achievement gap and equip all students in our changing society for success in jobs and the future challenges that await them. Developing countries are reinstituting the old industrial-style education system, which is no longer appropriate in the twenty-first century since information is available online and new generations of students are familiar with modern technology. According to Berry (2020), the current learning system is confined to institutions derived

from the bureaucratically organised twentieth-century school, which characterised teaching and learning as time and location bound.

One important SDG for education is Goal 4: 'to ensure inclusive and equitable quality education and promote lifelong learning opportunities for all'
(Rosa, 2017). In the education sector, 4IR technologies will play a major role
in instructional delivery and in providing support to the learners and teachers at
the same point in time (Rosa, 2017). The use of VR at the platform of
educational learning provides immersive and long-term retention while enhancing creativity through reinforced customisation of the stimulus (Bhattacharjee
et al., 2018). According to the World Economic Forum (2017), in order to
educate in the 4IR, instructors will need to use AI and robots, from which both
children and the teachers benefit dramatically.

15 Use of Technology during the COVID-19 Pandemic

As part of the 4IR, new technologies have made it easier to deal more effectively
with the speed, scope, and impact of the COVID-19 pandemic, such as AI for
medical treatment or mobile technology for data collection and contact tracing,
but these technologies aren't evenly available around the world, which has left
some underdeveloped and emerging countries and their vulnerable populations
at a big disadvantage. These 4IR technologies are already demonstrating their
ability to aid in the containment and management of the pandemic. Mobile
technologies and AI provide data-collecting tools that may be used to help in
contact tracing, symptom screening, and outbreak and vulnerability prediction.
Social distance is being assessed in public settings using AI-based computer
vision cameras, and AI-based thermal imaging cameras are being used to scan
public spaces and locate possibly ill persons all around the world, which is
concerning. Cloud-based platforms, as well as drones and robots, make it
simpler for employees to conduct social distancing by delivering medical
supplies to health facilities, as well as medicine and meals to infected patients,
among other things.

The potential to leverage these technologies in the battle against COVID-19
is not shared by all countries. Countries throughout the world have varying
levels of capacity, which relates to the physical and digital infrastructure, as well
as human capital, to make use of emerging technologies in general. Their use
and efficacy of 4IR technologies, which we refer to as the usage/effectiveness of
4IR technologies, likewise varies greatly among them.

Many countries have embraced the changes brought by the 4IR. Germany, for
example, has managed to keep its COVID-19 fatality rate far lower than that of
other European nations, and it is utilising location data from mobile phones to

conduct active contact-tracing efforts. With regard to South Korea, the Korea Centers for Disease Control and Prevention (KCDC) have developed a smartphone app for symptom reporting in addition to AI-powered chatbots and phone calls to distribute information and discover local testing sites. It is partly owing to the regulatory climate in South Korea that the country has been successful in implementing these technologies.

In the United States, health authorities have failed to increase the supply of critical medical supplies, and the public health response has been haphazard and disorganised in most cases. In contrast to other technologically sophisticated countries, the government was unable to conduct efficient digital contact-tracing activities in the United States. Furthermore, Spain has been chastised for failing to respond swiftly and decisively. Regulatory settings, privacy concerns, and organisational leadership all have an influence on how 4IR technologies are deployed to solve this global problem; hence, technological capability and utilisation cannot exist in a vacuum. These technologies are making it feasible for many people to continue working during lockdowns, and they are also helping to improve the medical response in times of emergency. However, the disparity between the haves and the have-nots continues to be enormous, both within and beyond countries. Investment, innovation, preparedness, and effective use and leadership within countries will be required to leverage the 4IR to combat COVID-19 so that no country and no one is left behind. Worldwide partnership and unity among nations will also be required to ensure broader access, usage, quality, and effectiveness of disruptive technologies for a healthier and more prosperous world.

15.1 Drone Technology during the COVID-19 Pandemic

Technologies of the 4IR are known to have too many moving parts owing to rapid advancements, policy requirements, and ambiguous end-user uptake. Drones are an ideal case study of this phenomenon. The development of safe and effective COVID-19 vaccines has been a huge step forward towards combating the pandemic, arresting the pan-world spread, bringing down the fatalities and the number of people getting infected. The R & D, including the production, is one vital part of the whole ambit of vaccination; equally important is the supply and distribution utilising the varied supply logistics chains, as is the administration of COVID vaccine jabs. The successful vaccination drive of any nation includes a three-pronged fight against COVID-19: that is, its prevention, surveillance, and containment.

Every technology available must be used, examining its viability for fighting COVID-19 and improving the situation worldwide. Technologies such as geospatial (an amalgamation of GIS, remote sensing, and GPS), AI, big data, telemedicine, blockchain, 5G, the Internet of Medical Things (IoMT), robotics, and unmanned aerial vehicles (UAV) or drones may well assist in combating COVID-19 for detecting, monitoring, diagnosing, screening, surveillance, tracking, mapping, sensitising, and creating awareness amongst the people.

UAVs or *drones* have been used sporadically to date in response to COVID-19. The applications and deployments of drones are for purposes such as delivering COVID vaccines and medicines; aerial spraying for decontamination of partially and fully contaminated areas; lab sample pickups and dropping of reports for reducing the time and exposure to infection; surveillance and monitoring of areas for controlling movement during lockdowns and quarantine; surveying inaccessible and dangerous areas; capturing the live administration of vaccination and relaying back to the health control centres.

Several sub-Saharan countries like Rwanda, Malawi, Ghana, and Sierra Leone have employed drones for delivery and transportation. A case in point is a company named Zipline, a drone delivery service that is utilising its experience and innovative technology to help deliver COVID-19 life-saving medications, blood products, and vaccines to patients in remote areas of Africa. It has also partnered with the government of Ghana to help deliver COVAX vaccines.

Another example is a corporate logistics giant based in Germany, DHL, which has been launching small drones that take off without needing a runway for launch. They are using these drones to deliver medications in coastal and other remote areas of the country. These drones also feature a temperature-controlled capacity unit that delivers the medications at their required temperature.

Drones can also act as a saviour in time-critical situations. In 2016, Google had also taken a step towards introducing a new device that could call for a drone in case of emergency with just the press of a button, saving the lives of many. The device can also play a vital role in delivering samples to laboratories that are far away from the collection areas.

India also launched its first-of-its-kind drone-driven aerial delivery facility to transport COVID vaccines and emergency medicines to inaccessible and difficult areas in the safest and fastest manner. Drone delivery of vaccines will go a long way to fulfilling the Prime Minister's '*Har Ghar Dastak*' campaign for a house-to-house vaccination drive. The district of Palghar in Maharashtra carried out an experiment to deliver COVID-19 vaccine doses to a remote village situated in rugged terrain. Also, a batch of 300 vaccines transported from Jawhar to Zaap village took just nine minutes, which otherwise would take more than forty minutes. Using drones for delivery purposes offsets the time and cost penalty if other means are used. It would be apt to call drones COVID warriors.

India's Universal Immunisation Programme is one of the largest in the world but vaccine logistics remains a challenge. Drones could play a key role in all the three fields of combating COVID-19 under this programme – prevention, surveillance, and containment. According to the WEF's global competitiveness report issued in 2019, India rated sixty-eighth overall (a ten-place drop) and fourth among the BRICS nations, with China placed first overall. In terms of the drone industry in India, the year 2021 brought about a slew of milestones that addressed this issue, from the liberalisation of drone policy to the near-instant commissioning of the flagship 'Medicine from the Sky' programme by the WEF, the Government of Telangana, Apollo Hospitals, and NITI Aayog: the SWAMITVA Yojana, which has the potential to be the largest drone survey in recorded history. All these programmes have provided an opportunity to use technology as a means of development, as well as providing health facilities to the remote areas of the country.

There are a few roadblocks in the use of drones for transportation and delivery, like the maintenance of ultra-cold temperatures for storing some of the COVID-19 vaccines creating logistical challenges. Even blood and serum are to be kept at specific temperatures. Another major roadblock is the lack of understanding of cases and scenarios where drone technology can add value in combating COVID-19.

The global medical drones market and the use of this technology are still in a nascent stage, amorphous and directionless. At present, drones are limited to pilot projects and short-term initiatives. The in-house manufacturing or the procurement and contracting mechanisms are major areas to be tackled under the framework of regulatory policies. The use of technology will be restricted unless a viable support system and enabling environment are built.

There will be a dire need for a trained and skilled workforce for drone operations. Education in this technology is a must for drone operators, government entities, and the end-users and medical professionals. Only thought-through policies from the government on the use and expansion of drone technology in the health sector and the integration with existing cutting-edge technologies will reap the maximum benefit to combat COVID-19 and only then will the impact be visible. When it comes to producing drones and drone components, as well as ancillary technologies, hardware, and 4IR technologies in general, the right strategy must be the primary emphasis.

'We've witnessed the equivalent of two years' worth of digital change in two months,' Satya Nadella stated. During COVID-19, consumers and businesses resorted to cloud computing, AI, the high speed of 5G networks, big data, and other technologies to expedite the adoption of 4IR technology. While many people and businesses were hesitant to commit completely to Industry 4.0 technologies at the time of the coronavirus pandemic, fortunately the capability and structure of such technologies were already in place, if not entirely polished.

16 Conclusion

> In the end, it all comes down to people and values. We need to shape a future that works for all of us by putting people first and empowering them. In its most pessimistic, dehumanized form, the Fourth Industrial Revolution may indeed have the potential to "robotize" humanity and thus deprive us of our hearts and soul. But as a complement to the best parts of human nature – creativity, empathy, stewardship – it can also lift humanity into a new collective and moral conscious-ness based on a shared sense of destiny. It is incumbent on us all to make sure the latter prevails.
>
> *(Schwab, 2015)*

Runde, Bandura, and Hammond (2019) suggest that, even though the 4IR will impact every nation, the measure of the impact will vary owing to differences in the demography and inherent challenges of individual nations. As a result, 4IR technologies and, by extension, 4IR reforms are being adopted to differing degrees across different industries and countries throughout the world. While some countries were early adopters of 4IR technologies and their changes, other countries were pessimistic about 4IR technologies and their changes, which resulted in a slowdown in the rate of adoption and changes.

The world has never been able to get enough of the ever-expanding new technologies. Today, the phrase 4IR refers to the fusion of currently existing cutting-edge technologies, their continuous upgradation, and the emerging tech-nologies which are presently being developed and projected to be widely avail-able in the next few years. It will revolutionise the volume of work (product and services) being handled, the speed with which it is produced or delivered, and the way it redefines itself based on the choices and preferences of the consumers.

There will be smart factories, smart machines, autonomous vehicles, intelli-gent robots, and the whole gamut of new technologies that will drastically transform the way we live, work, and interact with one another in the coming years and decades. There has never been anything like it in terms of magnitude, scope, and complexity in the history of the human race. No one knows exactly how it will evolve but one thing is certain: the approach must be coordinated and comprehensive, bringing together all players in the global political system, from the public and corporate sectors to academia and civil society.

At present, the emerging and the developing nations are lacking in network infrastructure, proper infrastructure, policy framework, and skilled workers to optimally tap the potential of the 4IR. The emerging economies have to work smartly to leapfrog them into the benefits of the 4IR and Industry 4.0. Risks and challenges will be encountered and public–private–people collaboration will be required to mitigate them.

Future technology advancements will also result in long-term advantages in efficiency and production. Reduced transportation and communication costs, more efficient logistics and global supply chains, and a reduction in trade expenses will all help open new markets and stimulate economic development. There is a lack of consensus about the best way to harness the recent developments of the 4IR; the emerging nations must produce visions and roadmaps to strengthen their competitive positions in the race.

A great deal of promise and a scary amount of risk are associated with the 4IR. At a time when advancements in computing power, biotechnologies, AI, renewable energies, additive manufacturing, and a slew of other emerging technologies are threatening to overwhelm us with their complexity, the 4IR concept is intended to assist individuals and organisations in making sense of the interplay between humans and technology. From self-driving cars to genetically altered people, the new millennium will provide technical and ethical challenges to industries, stakeholder groups, and societal norms throughout the spectrum.

The most essential effort in relation to the 4IR is not about further defining it but rather about understanding and influencing its influence on society. Four principles may be used to discuss the intersection of developing technology and international relations as a result of this:

The first step is to place an emphasis on systems rather than on the technologies themselves. In the meanwhile, although AI and blockchain continue to be hot topics, the most significant question is how to control these technologies as components of bigger systems rather than as standalone capabilities. Having a degree of 'minimum viable comprehension' of complicated, fast-moving issues as well as a desire to investigate the high-level social and political implications of future systems is required for this to be accomplished successfully.

The second step is to ensure that future technologies really empower, rather than direct, people in their everyday lives. As Jaron Lanier has pointed out, business models based on the manipulation of human behaviour on a large scale are fundamentally in conflict with individual liberties and national sovereignty conceptions, as well as with individual liberty principles (Fortson, 2018).

The third step is to behave jointly on purpose rather than by default. Given that we are still in the early stages of the 4IR, it is important to remember that the norms and standards, infrastructure, legislation, and business models that will define our future are still in the process of being established. Important choices regarding the future of our economies, political institutions, and communities must be negotiated and shared by a broad variety of responsible stakeholders, including governments, companies, and interest groups.

The fourth step is to see morals and ethics as an important aspect of technology systems, rather than as a nuisance to be avoided. Technologies are not, and never have been, only instruments of production. The absence of bias in any system is impossible because technologies impact through the biases they embed, both implicitly and openly, in the data they provide. Moreover, they exemplify the principles of their creators while simultaneously reflecting and constraining the aspirations of their consumers. It is necessary to address the ethical implications of technology at all phases of its development and application. This should be viewed as a practical, approachable, and necessary step in achieving the technology future that we desire. These four principles are intended to be prescriptive in nature.

The idea of 4IR is not and should not be interpreted as a simple attempt to represent the past, present, or future in a linear fashion. Essentially, it is a tool for delving deeply into the dynamics, values, stakeholders, and technologies of a fast-changing changing world and for pushing collective action inside and between nation-states in a manner that produces a more accessible, equitable, and successful society.

As the 4IR grows on top of the third, and new technologies emerge that make use of the global digital infrastructure to scale up, there will be a plethora of new methods to fulfil our dreams of the future. It is becoming increasingly difficult to distinguish between the digital world and the invisible fabric that we take for granted. The disruptive characteristics of a new world, reliant on cyberphysical systems, will necessitate new ways of thinking about technologies, thinking about ourselves, and thinking about how we govern collaboratively, wisely, and with the flourishing of humankind in mind.

Bibliography

Abdoola, S. (2019). Smart cities and the Fourth Industrial Revolution. Presentation at SAIEE Conference, Sandton International Conference Centre. Available at: https://az817975.vo.msecnd.net/wm-418498-cms images/ShafraazAbdool.pdf.

Adhikari, R. (2020). Fourth Industrial Revolution: from least developed countries to knowledge societies. In S. S. Aneel et al. (eds.), *Corridors of Knowledge for Peace and Development.* Sustainable Development Policy Institute, pp. 41–66, www.jstor.org/stable/resrep24374.13.

Ægisdóttir, A. L. (2016). Industry 4.0 & Made in China 2025. Available at: https://skemman.is/bitstream/1946/26101/4/Lokaritgerd%20-%20Industry%204.0%26Made%20in%20China%202025.pdf.

Aker, M. and Herrera, L. J. P. (2020). Smart literacy learning in the 21st century: facilitating PBSL pedagogic collaborative clouds. In S. Yu, M. Ally, and A. Tsinakos (eds.), *Emerging Technologies and Pedagogies in the Curriculum.* Singapore: Springer, pp. 429–46.

Ally, M. (2019). Competency profile of the digital and online teacher in future education. *International Review of Research in Open and Distributed Learning* 20(2): 302–18, https://doi.org/10.19173/irrodl.v20i2.4206.

Ally, M. and Wark, N. (2019, September). Learning for sustainable development in the Fourth Industrial Revolution. *Proceedings of the Pan-Commonwealth Forum 9 (PCF9), Commonwealth of Learning.* Available at: http://oasis.col.org/handle/11599/3393.

Ally, M. and Wark, N. (2019, November). Online education in the Fourth Industrial Revolution era. Paper presented at the International Council on Distance Education (ICDE), World Conference on Online Learning (WCOL) 2019, Dublin, Ireland. Available at: https://wcol2019.ie/wp-content/uploads/presentations/CP_052,%20ALLY.pdf.

Ally, M. and Wark, N. (2020). Sustainable development and education in the Fourth Industrial Revolution (4IR). Available at: http://oasis.col.org/bit stream/handle/11599/3698/2020_Ally_Wark_SustainDev_in_4IR.pdf?sequence=1

American Council for an Energy-Efficient Economy (2020). International energy efficiency scorecard. Available at: https://habitatx.com/wp-content/uploads/2016/07/2016_ACEEE_country_report.pdf.

Asghar, S., Rextina, G., Ahmed, T., and Tamimy, M. I. (2020). The Fourth Industrial Revolution in the developing nations: challenges and road map.

Commission on Science and Technology for Sustainable Development in the South Research Paper.

Asia-Pacific Economic Cooperation (2017). APEC 2017 high-level policy dialogue on human resources development in the digital age. Available at: www.apec.org:443/Meeting-Papers/Sectoral-Ministerial-Meetings/Human-Resources-Development/2017_hrd

Ayentimi, D. T. and Burgess, J. (2019). Is the fourth industrial revolution relevant to Sub-Sahara Africa? *Technology Analysis & Strategic Management* 31(6): 641–52.

Ayres, R. U. (1989). *Technological Transformations and Long Waves*. Vienna: Novographic.

Azoulay, A. (2018). Making the most of artificial intelligence. *The UNESCO Courier*, https://en.unesco.org/courier/2018-3/audrey-azoulaymaking-most-artificial-intelligence.

Bandyopadhyay, D. and Sen, J. (2011). Internet of Things: applications and challenges in technology and standardization. *Wireless Personal Communications* 58(1): 49–69.

Barker, K. (2021). How leaders are navigating a post-pandemic world. *People Matters*. Available at: www.peoplematters.in/article/leadership/how-leaders-are-navigating-a-post-pandemic-world-30259.

Berawi, M. A. (2018). Utilizing big data in industry 4.0: managing competitive advantages and business ethics. *International Journal of Technology* 3(1): 430–3.

Berry, J. E. (2020). The Internet: an educational system for equalizing educational opportunity. In R. Papa (ed.), *Handbook on Promoting Social Justice in Education*. Cham: Springer Nature, pp. 1587–1607.

Bhattacharjee, D., Paul, A., Kim, J. H., and Karthigaikumar, P. (2018). An immersive learning model using evolutionary learning. *Computers & Electrical Engineering* 65: 236–49, https://doi.org/10.1016/j.compeleceng.2017.08.023.

Bloem, J. et al. (2014). The Fourth Industrial Revolution: things to tighten the link between IT and OT. Available at: www.sogeti.com/globalassets/global/special/sogeti-things3en.pdf.

BloombergQuint. (n.d.). Modi's marquee schemes. Available at: www.bqprime.com/labs/modi-marquee-schemes/.

Bogoviz, A. V., Lobova, S. V., Ragulina, Y. V., and Alekseev, A. N. (2017). A comprehensive analysis of energy security in the member states of the Eurasian economic union, 2000–2014. *International Journal of Energy Economics and Policy* 7(5): 93–101.

Boyle, M. J. (2015). The legal and ethical implications of drone warfare. *The International Journal of Human Rights* 19(2): 105–26.

Bremicker, M. and Heynitz, H. V. (2016). *The Factory of the Future: Industry 4.0 – the Challenges of Tomorrow*. KPMG.

Breunig, M., Kelly, R., Mathis, R., and Wee, D. (2016). Industry 4.0 after the initial hype: where manufacturers are finding value and how they can best capture it. Available at: www.mckinsey.com/business/func tions/operations/our-insights/industry-40-looking-beyond-the-initial-hype.

Brynjolfsson, E. and McAfee, A. (2011). *Race against the Machine: How the Digital Revolution Is Accelerating Innovation, Driving Productivity, and Irreversibly Transforming Employment and the Economy*. Lexington, MA: Digital Frontier Press.

Buhr, D. (2015). Social innovation policy for Industry 4.0. Friedrich-Ebert-Stiftung, Division for Social and Economic Policies.

Cann, O. (2018). Machines will do more tasks than humans by 2025 but robot revolution will still create 58 million net new jobs in next five years. *World Economic Forum*. Available at: https://ideas4development.org/en/frugal-innovation-new-approach-pioneered-in-the-global-south/.

Chui, M., Manyika, J., and Miremadi, M. (2016). Where machines could replace humans – and where they couldn't (yet). Available at: www.mckin sey.com/business-functions/business-technology/ourinsights/where-machines-could-replace-humans-and-where-they-cant-yet.

Cissé, M. (2018). Democratizing AI in Africa. *The UNESCO Courier*. Available at: https://en.unesco.org/courier/2018-3/democratizing-ai-africa.

Condliffe, J. (2018). Strategies to cope with job-taking robots. *New York Times*, 9 June. www.nytimes.com/2018/07/09/business/dealbook/automation-devel oping-world.html.

Cotteleer, M. and Sniderman, B. (2017). Forces of change: Industry 4.0. *Deloitte Insights*, 18 December. Available at: www2.deloitte.com/insights/us/en/focus/industry-4-0/overview.html.

De le Rue du Can, S., Pudleiner, D., and Pielli, K. (2018). Energy efficiency as a means to expand energy access: a Uganda roadmap. *Energy Policy* 120: 354–64.

Deloitte Insights (2018). The Fourth Industrial Revolution is here: are you ready? Available at: www2.deloitte.com/content/dam/Deloitte/tr/Documents/manufacturing/Industry4-0_Are-you-ready_Report.pdf.

DESA, UN (United Nations Department of Economic and Social Affairs, Population Division) (2019). World population prospects. Available at: https://esa.un.org/unpd/wpp/.

Donovan, J. (2013). The 4th Industrial Revolution is upon us. Available at: www.ecnmag.com/article/2013/10/4th-industrial-revolution-upon-us.

Dutschke, E., Hirzel, S., Idrissova, F., Mielicke, U., and Nabitz, L. (2018). Energy efficiency networks – what are the processes that make them work? *Energy Efficiency* 11(5): 1177–95.

Esen, H. and Esen, M. (2017). Modelling and experimental performance analysis of solar assisted ground source heat pump system. *Journal of Experimental and Theoretical Artificial Intelligence* 29(1): 1–17.

Eyre, N. (1997). Barriers to energy efficiency: more than just market failure. *Energy and Environment* 8(1): 25–43, https://doi.org/10.1177/0958305x970 0800103.

Forbes India Magazine (2017). Going digital is the fourth industrial revolution. Available at: www.forbesindia.com/article/forbes-india-leaderspeak/going-digital-is-the-fourth-industrial-revolution/45395/1.

Ford, M. (2015). *Rise of the Robots: Technology and the Threat of a Jobless Future*. New York: Basic Books.

Fortson, D. (2018). Jaron Lanier's 10 reasons why you should delete your social media accounts right now. *The Times*, 20 May.

Gaspar, R., Antunes, D., Faria, A., and Meiszner, A. (2017). Sufficiency before efficiency: consumers' profiling and barriers/facilitators of energy efficient behaviours. *Journal of Cleaner Production* 165: 134–42, https://doi.org/10.1016/j.jclepro.2017.07.075.

Gereffi, G. (2014). Global value chains in a post-Washington Consensus world. *Review of International Political Economy* 21(1): 9–37.

Gereffi, G. (2015). Global Value Chains, development and emerging economies. Working Paper, United Nations. Available at: https://open.unido.org/api/documents/9924327/download/Global%20value%20chains%2C%20development%20and%20emerging%20economies.pdf.

Gereffi, G. (2018). *Global Value Chains and Development: Redefining the Contours of 21st-Century Capitalism*. Cambridge: Cambridge University Press.

Gereffi, G., Humphrey, J., and Sturgeon, T. (2005). The governance of global value chains. *Review of International Political Economy* 12(1): 78–104.

Golove, W. H. and Eto, J. H. (1996). *Market Barriers to Energy Efficiency: A Critical Reappraisal of the Rationale for Public Policies to Promote Energy Efficiency*. Berkeley, CA: Lawrence Berkeley National Laboratory.

Golpira, H. and Khan, S. A. R. (2019). A multi-objective risk-based robust optimization approach to energy management in smart residential buildings under combined demand and supply uncertainty. *Energy* 170: 1113–29. Available at: www.sciencedirect.com/science/article/abs/pii/S0360544218325593.

Goncharov, V. V. (2020). The Fourth Industrial Revolution: challenges, risks and opportunities. *Eruditio*, 13 September, http://eruditio.worldacademy.org/

volume-2/issue-6/article/fourth-industrial-revolution-challenges-risks-and-opportunities.

Goralskia, M. A. and Tan, T. K. (2020). Artificial intelligence and sustainable development. *International Journal of Management Education* 18: 1–9.

Habanik, J., Grencikova, A., and Krajco, K. (2019). The impact of new technology on sustainable development. *Engineering Economics* 30(1): 41–9, https://doi.org/10.5755/j01.ee.30.1.20776.

Hadjadj, R., Deak, C., Palotas, A. B., Mizsey, P., and Viskolcz, B. (2019). Renewable energy and raw materials – the thermodynamic support. *Journal of Cleaner Production* 241: 118221.

Haller, S., Karnouskos, S., and Schroth, C. (2008). The Internet of Things in an enterprise context. In *Future Internet Symposium*. Berlin: Springer, pp. 14–28.

Hewett, M. (1998). *Achieving Energy Efficiency in a Restructured Electric Utility Industry Prepared for Minnesotians and for Energy Efficiency Economy*. Center for Energy and Environment, Minneapolis, MN.

Hofmann, E., and Rüsch, M. (2017). Industry 4.0 and the current status as well as future prospects on logistics. *Computers in Industry* 89(1): 23–34.

Islam, M. A. and Jantan, A. H. (2017). The glass ceiling: career barriers for female employees in the Ready Made Garments (RMG) industry of Bangladesh. *Academy of Strategic Management Journal* 16(3), http://dx.doi.org/10.2139/ssrn.3414583.

Jaffe, A. and Stavins, R. (1994). The energy-efficiency gap: what does it mean? *Energy Policy* 22(10): 804–10, https://doi.org/10.1016/0301-4215(94)90138-4.

Joseph, N. A. and Nanjunga, T. (2020). The 4IR and financial inclusion in the age of Fintech. *Mmegi Online*, 26 June, www.mmegi.bw/opinion-analysis/the-4ir-and-financial-inclusion-in-the-age-of-fintech/news.

Kalaria, C. (2019). Industry 4.0: basic understanding and readiness of India. *Sourcing and Supply Chain*, 24 April, https://sourcingandsupplychain.com/industry-4-0-basic-understanding-and-readiness-of-india/.

Katzev, R. and Johnson, T. (1987). *Promoting Energy Conservation: An Analysis of Behavioural Approaches*. Boulder, CO: Westview Press.

Kay, J. (2021), Adam Smith and the Pin Factory. *Panmure House*. Available at: www.panmurehouse.org/perspectives/articles/adam-smith-and-the-pin-factory/.

Kollmuss, A. and Agyeman, J. (2002). Mind the gap: why do people act environmentally and what are the barriers to pro-environmental behavior? *Environmental Education Research* 8(3): 239–60.

Kounetas, K., Skuras, D., and Tsekouras, K. (2011). Promoting energy efficiency policies over the information barrier. *Information Economics and Policy* 23: 72–84.

Lai, M.-C., Wu, P.- 1., Liou, J.-L., Chen, Y., and Chen, H. (2019). The impact of promoting renewable energy in Taiwan – how much hail is added to snow in farmland prices? *Journal of Cleaner Production* 241: 118519.

Lasi, H., Fettke, P., Kemper, H., Feld, T., and Hoffmann, M. (2014). Industry 4.0. *Business & Information Systems Engineering* 6(1): 239–42.

Lee, K. (2013). *Schumpeterian Analysis of Economic Catch-up: Knowledge, Path-Creation, and the Middle-Income Trap.* Cambridge: Cambridge University Press.

Lee, K. (2018). How emerging economies can take advantage of the Fourth Industrial Revolution. Available at: www.weforum.org/agenda/2018/01/the-4th-industrial-revolution-is-a-window-of-opportunity-for-emerging-economies-to-advance-by-leapfrogging/.

Lee, K. (2019). *The Art of Economic Catch-up: Barriers, Detours and Leapfrogging in Innovation Systems.* Cambridge: Cambridge University Press.

Lee, K. (2021). How developing countries can take advantage of the Fourth Industrial Revolution. Available at: https://iap.unido.org/articles/how-devel oping-countries-can-take-advantage-fourth-industrial-revolution.

Lee, K. and Malerba, F. (2017). Catch-up cycles and changes in industry leadership: windows of opportunity and the responses by actors in sectoral systems. *Research Policy* 46(2): 338–51.

Lee, K., Malerba, F., and Primi, A. (2020). The Fourth Industrial Revolution, changing global value chains and industrial upgrading in emerging economies. *Journal of Economic Policy Reform* 23(4): 359–70, https://doi .org/10.1080/17487870.2020.1735386.

Lee, K., Szapiro, M., and Mao, Z. (2018). From global value chains (GVC) to innovation systems for local value chains and knowledge creation. *The European Journal of Development Research* 30(3): 424–41.

Lee, K., Wong, C.-Y., Intarakumnerd, P., and Limapornvanich, C. (2019). Is the 4th Industrial Revolution a window of opportunity for upgrading or reinforcing the middle-income trap? *Journal of Economic Policy Reform* 23(4): 408–25, https://doi.org/10.1080/17487870.2019.1565411.

Lihtmaa, L., Hess, D. B., and Leetmaa, K. (2018). Intersection of the global climate agenda with regional development: unequal distribution of energy efficiency-based renovation subsidies for apartment buildings. *Energy Policy* 119(32): 7–38.

Liu, P., Tuo, J., Liu, F., Li, C., and Zhang, X. (2018). A novel method for energy efficiency evaluation to support efficient machine tool selection. *Journal of Cleaner Production* 191: 57–66.

Loo, K. (2017). How the gig economy could drive growth in developing countries. *Forbes My Say*, 23 March. Available at: www.forbes.com/sites/

groupthink/2017/03/23/how-the-gig-economy-could-drive-growth-in-devel oping-countries/?sh=42181d9e4a49.

Lundvall, B.-Å. (1992). *National Systems of Innovation: Toward a Theory of Innovation and Interactive Learning*. London: Frances Pinter.

Lundvall, B.-Å. (2016). *The Learning Economy and the Economics of Hope*. London: Anthem Press.

Mahapatra, K., Alm, R., Hallgren, R., Yang, Y., and Umoru, I. (2018). A behavioral change-based approach to energy efficiency in a manufacturing plant. *Energy Efficiency* 11(5): 1103–16.

Maiorano, J. (2018). Beyond technocracy: forms of rationality and uncertainty in organizational behaviour and energy efficiency decision making in Canada. *Energy Research and Social Science* 44: 385–98, https://doi.org/ 10.1016/j.erss.2018.05.007.

Makridakis, S. (2017). The forthcoming Artificial Intelligence (AI) revolution: its impact on society and firms. *Futures* 90: 46–60, https://doi.org/10.1016/j .futures.2017.03.006.

Malerba, F. (2002). Sectoral systems of innovation and production. *Research Policy* 31(2): 247–64.

Martinelli, A., Mina, A., and Moggi, M. (2019). *The Enabling Technologies of Industry 4.0: Examining The Seeds of the Fourth Industrial Revolution*. Available at: https://siecon3-607788.c.cdn77.org/sites/siecon.org/files/media_ wysiwyg/257-martinelli.pdf.

Mavrikios, D., Alexopoulos, K., Georgoulias, K., Makris, S., Michalos, G., and Chryssolouris, G. (2019). Using holograms for visualizing and interacting with educational content in a Teaching Factory. *Procedia Manufacturing* 31: 404–10, https://doi.org/10.1016/j.promfg.2019.03.063.

Mavropoulos, A. (2016). Waste industry must prepare for 4th industrial revolu- tion. *ISWA Blog*. Available at: https://waste-management-world.com/a/iswa- blog-waste-industry-must-prepare-for-4th-industrial-revolution.

McGinnis, D. (2020). What is the Fourth Industrial Revolution? *Salesforce*, 27 October, www.salesforce.com/blog/what-is-the-fourth-industrial-revolu tion-4ir/.

Merriam, S. B. (1988) *Case Study Research in Education: A Qualitative Approach*. San Francisco: Jossey-Bass.

Middleton, C. (2018). Why China gains most from the Fourth Industrial Revolution – according to PwC. *Diginomica*, 24 September, https://digino mica.com/why-china-gains-most-from-the-fourth-industrial-revolution- according-to-pwc.

Miller, D. (2016). Natural language: the user interface for the Fourth Industrial Revolution. Opus Research Report. Available at: https://opusresearch.net/

wordpress/2016/11/04/opus-research-report-natural-language-the-user-inter face-for-the-fourth-industrial-revolution/.

Monivisal, T. (2020). Emerging technologies of the Fourth Industrial Revolution. *Cambodia Development Center* 2(8). Available at: https://cd-center.org/wp-content/uploads/2020/05/P127_20200520_V2IS8.pdf.

Naudé, W. (2017). Entrepreneurship, education and the Fourth Industrial Revolution in Africa. IZA Discussion Paper No. 10855. Available at: https://ssrn.com/abstract=2998964 or http://dx.doi.org/10.2139/ssrn.299 8964.

Nichols, A. (1994) Demand-side management overcoming market barriers or obscuring real costs? *Energy Policy* 22(10): 840–7, https://doi.org/10.1016/ 0301-4215(94)90143-0.

Njuguna, N. and Signe, L. (2020). The Fourth Industrial Revolution and digitization will transform Africa into a global powerhouse. Available at: www.brookings.edu/research/the-fourth-industrial-revolution-and-digitiza tion-will-transform-africa-into-a-global-powerhouse/.

OECD. (2019a). Scoping the OECD AI principles: deliberations of the expert group on artificial intelligence at the OECD (AIGO). OECD Digital Economy Papers, No. 291. Available at: https://doi.org/10.1787/d62f 618a-en.

OECD. (2019b). Artificial intelligence in society. OECD Publishing. Available at: https://doi.org/10.1787/eedfee77-en.

O'Halloran, D. and Kvochko, E. (2015). Industrial Internet of Things: unleash-ing the potential of connected products and services. World Economic Forum report. Available at: www.weforum.org/press/2015/01/industrial-internet-of-things-unleashing-the-potential-of-connected-products-and-services.

Parsa, A. (2018). The 4th Industrial Revolution and impact on urban develop-ment: the role of real estate. Available at: www.fig.net/resources/proceed ings/fig_proceedings/fig2018/ppt/PS01/1.2-Parsa.pdf.

Pates, D. (2020). The holographic academic: rethinking telepresence in higher education. In S. Yu, M. Ally, and A. Tsinakos (eds.), *Emerging Technologies and Pedagogies in the Curriculum*. Singapore: Springer, pp. 215–30.

Philbeck, T. and Davis, N. (2019). The Fourth Industrial Revolution: shaping a new era. *Journal of International Affairs* 72(1): 17–22.

Pollitzer, E. (2019). Creating a better future: four scenarios for how digital technologies could change the world. *Journal of International Affairs* 72(1): 75–90, www.jstor.org/stable/26588344.

Popkova, E. G., De Bernardi, P., Tyurina, Y. G., Sergi, B. S. (2022). A theory of digital technology advancement to address the grand challenges of sustain-able development. *Technology in Society* 68: 101831.

Popkova, E. G., Inshakova, A. O., Bogoviz, A. V., and Lobova, S. V. (2021). Energy efficiency and pollution control through ICTs for sustainable development. *Frontiers in Energy Research* 9: 735551.

Popkova, E. G. and Sergi, B. S. (2021). Energy efficiency in leading emerging and developed countries. *Energy* 221: 119730.

Popkova, E. G. and Zavyalova, E. (2021). Introduction: neo-institutional look at modern socio-economic development. In *New Institutions for Socio-Economic Development: The Change of Paradigm from Rationality and Stability to Responsibility and Dynamism*. Berlin: De Gruyter, pp. v–vi.

Porter, M. E. and Heppelmann, J. E. (2014). How smart, connected products are transforming competition. *Harvard Business Review* 92(11): 64–88.

Primi, A. and Toselli, M. (2020). A global perspective on Industry 4.0 and development: new gaps or opportunities to leapfrog? *Journal of Economic Policy Reform* 23(4): 371–89, https://doi.org/10.1080/17487870.2020.1727322.

Proskuryakova, L. and Filippov, S. (2015). Energy technology foresight 2030 in Russia: an outlook for safer and more efficient energy future. *Energy Procedia* 75: 2798–806, https://doi.org/10.1016/j.egypro.2015.07.550.

Reddy, K. and Sasidharan, S. (2021). A portrait of global value chain linkages of Indian manufacturing. *Journal of Asian Economic Integration* 3(2), September: 235–50, https://doi.org/10.1177/26316846211039419.

Rohdin, P. and Thollander, P. (2006). Barriers to and driving forces for energy efficiency in the non-energy intensive manufacturing industry in Sweden. *Energy* 31(12): 1836–44, https://doi.org/10.1016/j.energy.2005.10.010.

Rosa, W. (ed.). (2017). Transforming our world: the 2030 agenda for sustainable development. In *A New Era in Global Health*. Available at: https://doi.org/10.1891/9780826190123.ap02.

Rotatori, D., Lee, E. J., and Sleeva, S. (2021). The evolution of the workforce during the Fourth Industrial Revolution. *Human Resource Development International* 24(1): 92–103, https://doi.org/10.1080/13678868.2020.1767453.

Rubin, A. and Brown, A. (2019). Unlocking the future of learning by redesigning educator learning. In J. W. Cook (ed.), *Sustainability, Human Well-Being, and the Future of Education*. Cham: Springer Nature, pp. 235–68.

Rudge, P. (2019). Small island developing states and the fourth industrial revolution. United Nations Conference on Trade and Development. Available at: https://unctad.org/meetings/en/Contribution/cep2019-29.10-contribution_PRudge_SIDS_UK.pdf.

Runde, D., Bandura, R., and Hammond, M. (2019). *Making the Future Work for Us: Technological Impacts on Labor in the Developing World*. Washington, DC: Center for Strategic & International Studies.

Rüßmann, M., Lorenz, M., Gerbert, P., Waldner, M., Justus, J., Engel, P., and Harnisch, M. (2015). Industry 4.0: The future of productivity and growth in manufacturing industries. *Boston Consulting Group* 9(1): 54–89.

Safarzadeh, S. and Rasti-Barzoki, M. (2019). A game theoretic approach for pricing policies in a duopolistic supply chain considering energy productivity, industrial rebound effect, and government policies. *Energy* 167: 92–105.

Sardianou,E. (2008). Barriers to industrial energy efficiency investments in Greece. *Journal of Cleaner Production* 16(13): 1416–23, https://doi.org/10.1016/j.jclepro.2007.08.002.

Sage Metals (2019). Indian Manufacturing Industry has a shining future. Available at: https://sagemetals.com/indian-manufacturing-industry-has-a-shining-future/.

Schwab, K. (2015). The Fourth Industrial Revolution: what it means and how to respond. Available at: www.foreignaffairs.com/articles/2015-12-12/fourth-industrial-revolution.

Schwab, K. (2016). The Fourth Industrial Revolution. Geneva: World Economic Forum.

Schwab, K. (2017). *The Fourth Industrial Revolution*. London: Portfolio Penguin.

Schwab, K. (2018a). Globalization 4.0: shaping a global architecture in the age of the Fourth Industrial Revolution. A report for the Annual Meeting of the Global Future Councils, Dubai.

Schwab, K. (2018b). Globalization 4.0 – what it means and how it could benefit us all. World Economic Forum Agenda, 5 November. Available at: www.weforum.org/agenda/2018/11/globalization-4-what-does-it-mean-how-it-will-benefiteveryone/.

Schwab, K. (2019). Foreword. *Journal of International Affairs* 72(1): 13–16, www.jstor.org/stable/26588338.

Schwab, K. and Davis, N. (2018). *Shaping the Fourth Industrial Revolution*. New York: Currency.

Senate of the Italian Republic. (2017). The impact of the fourth Insutrial Revolution on the jobs market. Available at: www.bollettinoadapt.it/wp-content/uploads/2017/11/the-impact-of-the-fourth-industrial-revolution-on-the-jobs-market.pdf.

Sergi, B. S. and Popkova, E. G. (2022). Towards a 'wide' role for venture capital in OECD countries' Industry 4.0. *Heliyon* 8(1): e08700.

Seric, A. and Tong, Y. S. (2019). What are Global Value Chains and why do they matter. *Industrial Analytics Platform*. Available at: https://iap.unido.org/articles/what-are-global-value-chains-and-why-do-they-matter.

Siddiqui, O., Dincer, I., Yilbas, B. S. (2019). Development of a novel renewable energy system integrated with biomass gasification combined cycle for cleaner production purposes. *Journal of Cleaner Production* 241: 118345.

Singh, A. and Prasad Painuly, J. (2009). Financing energy efficiency: lessons from experiences in India and China. *International Journal of Energy Sector Management* 3(3): 293–307, https://doi.org/10.1108/17506220910986815.

Smeets, M. (2021). Converging thoughts on digital trade in preparing for the future. World Trade Organization. Available at: www.wto.org/english/res_e/booksp_e/20_adtera_chapter_16_e.pdf.

Soh, C. and Connolly, D. (2021). New frontiers of profit and risk: the Fourth Industrial Revolution's impact on business and human rights. *New Political Economy* 26(1): 168–85, https://doi.org/10.1080/13563467.2020.1723514.

Sudhakara Reddy, B. (2013). Barriers and drivers to energy efficiency – a new taxonomical approach. *Energy Conversion and Management* 74: 403–416, https://doi.org/10.1016/j.enconman.2013.06.040.

Sutherland, R. J. (1991). Market barriers to energy-efficiency investments. *Energy Journal* 12(3), https://doi.org/10.5547/ISSN0195-6574-EJ-Vol12-No3-3.

Thomas, T. (2022). Economic survey 2022: R&D key to transitioning to clean energy. *Money Control*, 31 January. Available at: www.moneycontrol.com/news/business/economy/economic-survey-2022-rd-key-to-transitioning-to-clean-energy-8009231.html.

Thompson, P. (1997). Evaluating energy efficiency investments: accounting for risk in the discounting process. *Energy Policy* 25(12): 989–96, https://doi.org/10.1016/s0301-4215(97)00125-0.

Timilsina, G., Hochman, G., and Fedets, I. (2016). Understanding energy efficiency barriers in Ukraine: insights from a survey of commercial and industrial firms. *Energy* 106: 203–11, https://doi.org/10.1016/j.energy.2016.03.009.

Trappey, A. J., Trappey, C. V., Govindarajan, U. H., Chuang, A. C., and Sun, J. J. (2017). A review of essential standards and patent landscapes for the Internet of Things: a key enabler for industry 4.0. *Advanced Engineering Informatics* 33(1): 208–29.

UN (2015). Transforming our world: the 2030 agenda for sustainable development. Available at: https://sustainabledevelopment.un.org/post2015/transformingourworld.

UN (2020). Goals in the sphere of sustainable development 2020. Available at: www.un.org/sustainbledevelopmet/ru/sustainable-development-goals/.

UNCTAD (2013). *Global Value Chains: Investment and Trade for Development*. World Investment Report. New York & Geneva: UNCTAD.

UNCTAD (2017). Robots, industrialization and inclusive growth. Chapter 3 of *Trade and Development Report*. Geneva: UNCTAD.

UNESCO (2019). Meeting commitments: are countries on track to achieve SDG4? Available at: https://reliefweb.int/sites/reliefweb.int/files/resources/UNESCO-2019-HLPF_UIS_Meeting-EN-v7-web_aer.pdf.

USDOE (US Department of Education) (1983). *A Nation at Risk: The Imperative for Educational Reform*. Washington, DC: US Government Printing Office. Available at: www.edreform.com/wp-content/uploads/2013/02/A_Nation_At_Risk_1983.pdf.

Vaninsky, A. (2018). Energy-environmental efficiency and optimal restructuring of the global economy. *Energy* 153: 338–48.

Vikas, N. (2018). India's leap towards a sustainable Fourth Industrial Revolution. *The CSR Journal*, 7 July, https://thecsrjournal.in/leap-sustainable-fourth-industrial-revolution/.

Vincent-Lancrin, S. and van der Vlies, R. (2020). Trustworthy artificial intelligence (AI) in education: promises and challenges. OECD Education Working Paper, No. 218, https://doi.org/10.1787/a6c90fa9-en.

Wang, H., Pan, C., Wang, Q., and Zhou, P. (2020). Assessing sustainability performance of global supply chains: an input-output modeling approach. *European Journal of Operational Research* 285(1): 393–404, https://doi.org/10.1016/j.ejor.2020.01.057.

Wei, Y.-M. and Liao, H. (1993). Energy efficiency in developed model to compare energy-efficiency indices and CO2 emissions in developed and developing countries. *Energy Policy* 21(3): 276–83, https://doi.org/10.1016/0301-4215(93)90249-f.

Witkowski, K. (2017). Internet of things, big data, industry 4.0: innovative solutions in logistics and supply chains management. *Procedia Engineering* 182(1): 763–9.

Wohlfarth, K., Eichhammer, W., Schlomann, B., and Worrell, E. (2018). Tailoring cross-sectional energy-efficiency measures to target groups in industry. *Energy Efficiency* 11(5): 1265–79.

Wood, A. J., Lehdonvirta, V., and Graham, M. (2018). Workers of the Internet unite? Online freelancer organisation among remote gig economy workers in six Asian and African countries. *New Technology, Work and Employment* 33(2): 95–112.

World Bank (2010). *Exploring the Middle-Income-Trap, East Asia Pacific Economic Update*. Washington, DC: World Bank, vol. 2.

World Economic Forum (2017). Realizing human potential in the Fourth Industrial Revolution: an agenda for leaders to shape the future of education, gender and work. White paper, www3.weforum.org/docs/WEF_EGW_Whitepaper.pdf.

World Economic Forum (2020a). Centre for the Fourth Industrial Revolution, www.weforum.org/centre-for-the-fourth-industrial-revolution/.

World Economic Forum (2020b). India Centre for the Fourth Industrial Revolution. https://weforum.ent.box.com/v/C4IR-India.

World Energy Council (2020). Energy efficiency indicators. Available at: https://wec-indicators.enerdata.net/world.php.

Yang, L., Wang, K.-L., and Geng, J.-C. (2018). China's regional ecological energy efficiency and energy saving and pollution abatement potentials: an empirical analysis using epsilon-based measure model. *Journal of Cleaner Production* 194: 300–8.

Yang, Y. (2019). China takes a leading role in Fourth Industrial Revolution, *China Daily*, www.chinadaily.com.cn/a/201907/11/WS5d26cb19a3105895c2e7cee3 .html.

Zakaria, F. (2015). Why America's obsession with STEM education is dangerous. *Washington Post*, March.

Zeng, S., Liu, Y., Liu, C., and Nan, X. (2017). A review of renewable energy investment in the BRICS countries: history, models, problems and solutions. *Renewable and Sustainable Energy Reviews* 74: 860–72, https://doi.org/ 10.1016/j.rser.2017.03.016.

Zhao, M., Deng, D., Zhou, W., and Fan, L. (2018). Non-renewable energy efficiency optimization in energy harvesting relay-assisted system. *Physical Communication* 29: 183–90.

About the Authors

Dr Mark Esposito is recognised internationally as a top global thought leader in matters relating to the Fourth Industrial Revolution, the changes and opportunities that technology will bring to a variety of industries. He is co-founder and Chief Learning Officer at Nexus FrontierTech, an AI scale-up venture, and co-founder and Chairman of the Strategic Foresight Board for the Circular Economy Alliance, an EdTech venture. He was inducted in 2016 into the Radar of Thinkers50 as one of the thirty most prominent rising business thinkers in the world. He is a global expert of the World Economic Forum, an advisor to national governments, and a Distinguished Fellow in the UNESCO Chair in Future Literacy of Finance. He is currently an advisor for the Prime Minister's Office in the UAE. He contributed to six reports for the World Economic Forum and co-authored a policy brief for the Brookings Institution in the field of governance of technology. He serves as Senior Advisor to the Ideation Center of Strategy and at PwC in Dubai since April 2022.

He is Professor of Business and Economics at Hult International Business School and faculty at Harvard University's Division of Continuing Education. He served as Institutes Council Co-Leader of the Microeconomics of Competitiveness program (MOC) at the Institute of Strategy and Competitiveness, Harvard Business School under the mentorship of Professor Michael E. Porter. He holds a Clinical Professorship at Arizona State University's Thunderbird where he also has a Faculty Fellowship at the Sandra O'Connor Law School. He was also at Judge Business School, University of Cambridge from 2016 to 2020 as Founding Fellow for the Circular Economy Centre.

He has authored or co-authored over 150 publications (peer and non-peer reviewed) and 11 books, among which are 2 Amazon bestsellers: *Understanding How the Future Unfolds* (2017) and *The AI Republic* (2019). His next book, *The Great Remobilization: Designing a Smarter World*, will be published by MIT University Press, in early 2023.

He holds a doctoral degree in Business and Economics from École des Ponts ParisTech, one of France's most prestigious Grandes Écoles.

Amit Kapoor, PhD, is Honorary Chairman at the Institute for Competitiveness, India, President of the India Council on Competitiveness, and Editor-in-Chief of Thinkers. He is the chair of the Social Progress Imperative and Shared Value Initiative in India. He is an affiliate faculty for the Microeconomics of Competitiveness and Value-Based Health Care Delivery courses at the

Institute of Strategy and Competitiveness, Harvard Business School and an instructor with Harvard Business Publishing in the area of Strategy, Competitiveness and Business Models in addition to being a visiting scholar and lecturer at Stanford University, where he teaches a course on rebalancing economic systems and rethinking economics.

He has been inducted into the Competitiveness Hall of Fame which is administered by the Institute for Strategy and Competitiveness at Harvard Business School in addition to being the recipient of the Ruth Greene Memorial Award for writing the best case of the year, by the North American Case Research Association (NACRA).

Amit is the author of bestsellers *Riding the Tiger*, which he co-authored with Wilfried Aulber, and *The Age of Awakening: The Story of the Indian Economy Since Independence*, published by Penguin Random House. His recent book *Disrupting Democracies* is published by the Bertelsmann Foundation.

He is also a columnist with *Economic Times* and *Business World*, and in addition his contributions have been published by *Harvard Business Review Online*, *Hindu*, *Business Insider*, *Hindu Business Line*, *Mint*, *Financial Express*, *Outlook Business*, *Governance Now*, *Business Today*, and *FirstPost*, among others. In all, he has written over 600 opinion pieces apart from publishing academic research (cases and articles). Based on his work, three awards have been constituted within the country, titled State Competitiveness Awards, wherein the Chief Ministers are awarded; City Competitiveness Awards, wherein City Heads are awarded; and Institute for Competitiveness Strategy Awards, wherein the corporates are awarded for their strategic acumen. He chairs the jury and curates the Porter Prize in addition to curating events like National Competitiveness Forum, Shared Value Summit, and Thinkers50 (India).

Cambridge Elements ☰

Economics of Emerging Markets

Bruno S. Sergi
Harvard University

Editor Bruno S. Sergi is an Instructor at Harvard University, an Associate of the Harvard University Davis Center for Russian and Eurasian Studies and Harvard Ukrainian Research Institute. He is the Academic Series Editor of the Cambridge *Elements in the Economics of Emerging Markets* (Cambridge University Press), a co-editor of the *Lab for Entrepreneurship and Development* book series, and associate editor of *The American Economist*. Concurrently, he teaches International Economics at the University of Messina, Scientific Director of the Lab for Entrepreneurship and Development (LEAD), and a co-founder and Scientific Director of the International Center for Emerging Markets Research at RUDN University in Moscow. He has published over 150 articles in professional journals and twenty-one books as author, co-author, editor, and co-editor.

About the Series
The aim of this Elements series is to deliver state-of-the-art, comprehensive coverage of the knowledge developed to date, including the dynamics and prospects of these economies, focusing on emerging markets' economics, finance, banking, technology advances, trade, demographic challenges, and their economic relations with the rest of the world, as well as the causal factors and limits of economic policy in these markets.

Cambridge Elements ⌘

Economics of Emerging Markets

Elements in the Series

A full series listing is available at: www.cambridge.org/EEM

Printed in the United States
by Baker & Taylor Publisher Services